DISCIPLINE
that CONNECTS
with Your
CHILD'S HEART

DISCIPLINE
that CONNECTS
with Your
CHILD'S HEART

JIM AND LYNNE JACKSON

Connected Families
566 Bavaria Lane
Chaska, MN 55318

To order this book please visit www.connectedfamilies.org

ISBN 978-0-9849942-0-5
eBook 978-0-9849942-1-2

Unless otherwise noted, Scriptures taken from the NEW INTERNATIONAL VERSION, Copyright © 1973, 1978, 1984 by International Bible Society. Used by permission of Zondervan. All rights reserved.

For information on other materials by Jim & Lynne Jackson contact Connected Families Ministries at 566 Bavaria Lane, Chaska, MN – or at www.connectedfamilies.org

Front Cover Design by Kitt Wichmann - http://www.studiokitt.com
Back cover and book Layout Design by Sarah O'Neal | www.evecustomartwork.com
Cover Photo courtesy of iStockphoto
Printed by Snowfall Press
www.snowfallpress.com

Printed in the United States of America

Contents

Dear Readers

In this book you'll learn a profound and powerful approach for discipline in God's love, grace and truth. We call this approach "Discipline that Connects." Families who live joyfully, gracefully, and with respect for God's Word know these principles, even if they didn't learn them from us. God invented great parenting, after all. We have just organized these Biblical ideas in a way that is easy to remember, so that you will be inspired and equipped for wise, loving, and graceful discipline. When you keep working toward applying the things you'll learn here, you will stay well connected to your children, your kids' hearts will be soft and open to relationship with God, and your family will be a blessing to others.

Our kids need this. Our world needs this.

Chapter 1

"I'm Hoping He'll Learn His Lesson"

Karla was fed up. "My son Nathan has been nothing but trouble lately! Every day after school he just drops his backpack in the entry and goes off to his computer obsession. When I confront him for playing computer games before doing his homework, he sasses at me and storms off. He even swears. So I've grounded him from the computer and from going outside. Sometimes I work hard at setting consequences to make this stop. Other times I feel so tired I just let him go. Just yesterday he had a huge meltdown about it, but this can't keep happening. He's gotta learn!" Karla was at once exhausted, irate, overwhelmed and looking for answers.

"What are you hoping he'll learn?" I (Jim) asked.

"I'm hoping he'll learn his lesson," she replied.

"And what lesson is that?"

"That getting away with that kind of disrespect in this house just isn't gonna' happen." She sounded a bit defiant herself.

"And how well do you think he's learning it?"

"That's the problem," she was quick to respond. "It seems the harder I try, the worse he gets. I used to spank him, but it just made him madder. So I've tried timeouts; I take away his iPod or computer; I ground him. Sometimes I just ignore it and hope it will go away. But nothing I do connects with him. None of it works."

Karla in one sweeping story described the two extremes parents often live in that illustrate the big problem with discipline. Either they put a tight and controlling grip on their kids in order to prevent misbehavior, or they give up trying because it's too hard or they are too tired or preoccupied. They often go back and forth between these extremes, hoping to get their kids to behave.

When parents approach discipline in these ways, the children usually don't learn the lessons the parents want to teach. So the discipline does not "connect." Instead, it leads to a snowballing cycle of arguments, frustration, and defiance that ultimately gives kids a sense that they are in charge of their parents' emotions, and that their parents are not really respectable.

> These simple but profound ideas guide parents to act in new ways—to think, act, and love more in alignment with God's heart for discipline.

Parents then work harder to find the new fix, the new formula, the new book, audio series, or online resource that will equip them to teach children "their lesson." But they do little work to understand what's really going on inside themselves and their children, and little work to connect spiritual truth to the discipline effort.

Discipline that connects with your child's heart is powerfully different. Centered in four biblical principles, we have seen the "Discipline that Connects" approach absolutely transform the discipline experience of the parents who embrace these principles. And when discipline is transformed, the whole relationship is better. These simple but profound ideas guide parents to act in new ways—to think, act, and love more in alignment with God's heart for discipline.

When parents commit to learning these principles, they often see dramatic improvements in their relationship with their children.

But even if changes in children's behavior come slowly, the parents learn to be peaceful and confident in their efforts, driven more by what's best for each child than by the urgency of the moment. At the very least, children will know that their parents are different, and over time, when parents are calm, confident and grounded in a sense of peace and purpose, they are better positioned to influence their children toward a better way.

Let's look at how the "Discipline that Connects" principles might guide the situation Karla described above:

Karla noticed the unopened backpack in the front hall and heard the noises of a computer game in Nathan's room. She started to get angry because he was again disobeying by playing computer games before doing his homework, but she recognized her familiar angst and knew it would lead to an ugly power struggle. She also recognized that some of her anger was probably due to left-over stress from her own day. So she slowed her pace, took a deep breath and prayed, "Lord, you love this kid and so do I. I need your wisdom now to deal with this. Help me have a forgiving rather than an accusing spirit."

She went in to Nathan and, sure enough, he was gaming on the computer. She gently put her hand on his shoulder and sat down next to him. In a firm but nonthreatening tone she started, "Honey, do you remember what I asked you to do before playing computer games?" He shrugged. She continued, calm but confident, "I know you love this game, but I want to make sure you're listening when I explain the consequence for playing it before doing your home-work." She paused, hoping he might stop on his own, but he didn't. Karla continued, her tone raising slightly, "Your persistence here is something God can use some day; it's just not helpful right now. If you pause the game immediately you can get back on again after your homework is done, but if not, then I'll decide how long it will be before you can play again."

Nathan hit the pause button and looked grudgingly over at her. "What's the big deal?"

Karla softened. "I appreciate your attention. The big deal is that you're disobeying me again by playing this game before doing your homework." Nathan took a quick breath, the kind that Karla knew would lead to a complaint. She anticipated this and quickly continued. "I can see you're really good at that game, and it seems to tempt you away from your responsibilities." Karla paused, wanting that statement to sink in a bit, and thinking about a way to empathise with Nathan. She felt sure of herself and continued, "That kind of thing happens to me sometimes too. We could talk about that for a moment, or we could get right to talking about your homework and computer games—what's your preference?" In this one sentence Karla had brilliantly offered two choices and put an important decision in Nathan's court without compromising her parental role—and with a touch of empathy too.

"Whatever." Nathan was off balance. Where usually he just fought the consequences, Karla's discipline was opening him to listen and learn because she was kind but confident in her authority. Nathan didn't really listen to the choices offered, but neither did he feel defensive or trapped. Where usually Karla was angry or exasperated, thus exasperating Nathan by her efforts, Karla was now in control of herself, and Nathan was feeling the weight of his own choices. His response surprised Karla a bit. "I just hate my math teacher, and the homework is stupid. It's so confusing, and I'm never gonna use that stuff in real life!"

"Ahh, I get it," Karla empathized. She'd landed on the root of his homework avoidance. She responded not with a lecture or judgement, but with a simple rephrasing of what she'd heard. "Things a little tough at school right now?"

"Yeah. No kidding." Nathan's gaze moved to the floor.

"Sounds like you're pretty frustrated and discouraged. I can help you get started on your math now. Over dinner let's figure out what could help you feel better about math and follow the rules about homework." Nathan, while not by any means enthused, was now open. Karla's discipline had connected.

By these efforts, Karla set the stage for a constructive process of coming alongside Nathan as a guide. Instead of getting locked in a power struggle she couldn't win, she created a safe space for Nathan to share his discouragement. Instead of being against him, she was *with* him in his struggle. She gained respect, kept her position of authority and reached a helpful, purposeful solution. This scenario illustrates one way that the "Discipline that Connects" principles have helped hundreds of parents actually strengthen their influence and bond with their children in the kind of discipline situations that often drive families apart.

Typical Discipline Misses the Mark

When misbehavior happens, one of two things typically happen. The first is that parents charge in without thinking and deal with children as if they are problems to be fixed. Parents often have a primary goal: "This behavior should stop—now." Underneath this goal may be unidentified but powerful feelings of anxiety, anger, embarrassment, and confusion. Because of these intense emotions, parents become demanding. We tend to get loud. We're prone to irrational or even hurtful words and tactics in our efforts to win. If winning equates to gaining immediate control, these tactics can be effective—at least for a season. But no one really wins when this is the typical discipline, because kids either comply in order to stay out of trouble or they rebel against the control. Once out from under the controlling parent, these kids typically lose control of themselves because they've never learned to be self-guided.

The other typical response is that parents give in or give up. They let the kids get away with various misbehavior because it's just too hard to "win," especially as the kids get older. These parents pick up the messes and turn their back on conflicts with a goal of keeping the peace and not offending their kids. They tend to feel weak and hurt. They fear conflict and the rejection from their children that can come with it. These parents often express that they feel like doormats, or that their kids just don't appreciate them. Their kids grow up feeling entitled to get what they want.

Even the "best" of parents will report sometimes getting stuck in these extremes of either dominating control or passive avoidance. But when parents set the goal of being sure their discipline connects with their children's hearts, they can little by little (and sometimes, in "aha" moments, really quickly) change their approach in powerful and lasting ways. These parents grow to profoundly influence not just their children's behavior, but their hearts. This is what Discipline that Connects does.

Our hope and prayer is that as you grow into an understanding of the Discipline that Connects principles, you will set goals for discipline that go far (really far!) beyond just controlling or avoiding you child's misbehavior. We pray that your goal for discipline will be to model God's grace, truth and love in even the messiest of discipline challenges. Whether you do this in the midst of the discipline, or in heart-felt reconciliation if you've "missed the mark," we know that living according to this goal will have a profound impact on your children as they see faith come alive in your home.

Discipline puts to the test what we most deeply believe. Is Christ's love longer, wider, higher and deeper than our children's (and our) misbehavior? Is his mercy present in our ugly conflicts, drawing our hearts back together? Does God's Word truly bring valuable, protective wisdom to get us back on track when we sin? Is the Holy Spirit's power more than sufficient to keep us growing in faith and character when we struggle? Simply stated, *it is in discipline that our efforts to disciple our children to love and follow God can become vibrantly real.* If our kids attend church and participate in Sunday school and youth group, but we continue to discipline our kids in typical ways, they likely will conclude that the great spiritual principles of the Christian life do not really reach into the deepest part of our lives.

For discipline to be effective in discipleship, it must flow from a parent's heart of humility, forgiveness, wisdom, love, and vision for a child's life. It must make sense to the child and win the child's respect. We ultimately know that discipline has connected with a child's heart when the child develops a desire to know and love Jesus, and to walk in the grace of obedience to him. That is the goal this book is ultimately about.

SECTION ONE: THE PREPARED HEART

Chapter 2

Preparing My Heart

What follows is a brief overview of the four "Discipline that Connects" principles. It is our hope that by the end of this book you'll have an imprint of these ideas on your heart and in your mind. We pray that they will equip you to reach a goal of discipline that connects with the hearts of your children in life-changing ways.

I Prepare My Heart

The first principle is about me, the parent. If I want my discipline to connect, I have some work to do *before* I engage with my child. I prepare my heart. I am thoughtful about my goals for discipline so that in the heat of the moments, when my child is defiant, or whining, or lying, or messy, or all of the above, I am guided by more than the need of the moment. Then when the moments come, preparing my heart might be about taking a breath. It might be about saying a prayer. Perhaps I'll take a step back instead of charging in. Maybe I'll learn to think about the opportunity for learning rather than the problem to be corrected. I let go of my goal to just make the problem go away as quickly as possible. I remember my guiding goal of modeling God's grace and forgiveness. Essentially, I do whatever I need to do to calm down and enter the situation focused on what my child really needs. It's amazing what a difference it can make when I keep myself calm and rational as I discipline my child. In the previous story:

- Karla was aware of her difficult emotions, what was causing

- them and what would happen if anxiety and anger drove her responses to Nathan.
- She took a breath and waited to engage Nathan until she was calm enough to remember her love for him and had some wisdom and insight into how to respond well.
- She prayed for wisdom and asked for a spirit of forgiveness.

When I prepare well for discipline, I can focus on my ultimate goals for the discipline. As one person wisely observed, "It's a long day on the golf course if you don't know where the hole is." It can be a "long day" of repeated, frustrating discipline incidents, especially if you don't really know what you are trying to accomplish. Parents who have thoughtfully developed goals are more confident and effective, and less fearful or volatile. Consider these three following principles as you develop your convictions and goals for discipline. The principles are in the form of key messages to communicate to your children - "You are LOVED, You are CAPABLE, and You are RESPONSIBLE."

"You Are LOVED (no matter what)"

"Sure," some parents say, "I show my kids love when they misbehave—tough love, the kind that hurts me more than it hurts them." Sometimes there certainly is merit in firm and strong discipline measures as one element of loving discipline. But if that's all my children ever receive from me when they misbehave, then they are not getting a balanced experience of God's heart for misbehaving people. We know from experience that it's easy to justify strong and punitive discipline from an angry heart, but very rarely is it delivered from a heart of forgiveness and grace.

Other parents show kids "love" by letting their kids off the hook. Again, there may sometimes be reasons parents want to show some mercy, but if parents habitually ignore or don't hold kids accountable for misbehavior, the kids aren't drawn into the Biblical truth that "God cannot be mocked. A man (or child) reaps what he sows!" These kids don't learn to take responsibility for their own actions. So the key is to show love in ways that holds kids accountable for learning without exasperating them.

In 1 John 3:1 we're told about the nature of God's love—it is lavished. Through thick and thin, through good and bad, through belief and disbelief, God's love is persis-

> Imagine if our first goal in discipline challenges was to respond as a three-dimensional demonstration of Christ's love—even when our children act up.

tent and pervasive to the point of being overwhelming. Romans 5:8 says it this way, "God demonstrates his own love for us in this: While we were still sinners..." (filled with disobedience, defiance, disbelief, and every kind of misbehavior) "...Christ died for us." Imagine if our first goal in discipline challenges was to respond as a three-dimensional demonstration of Christ's love—even when our children act up. It's like this:

- When Karla saw Nathan at the computer, she sat next to him and put her hand on his shoulder.
- She spoke in a gentle voice and kept the interaction lighthearted.
- She started with empathy rather than an ultimatum and admitted that fun activities sometimes tempt her away from responsibilities too.

- She was understanding when he expressed his frustration with math.

When this kind of love shows up during a time of disciplining, a child's rigid defiance tends to melt like ice on sun-warmed pavement. It doesn't let kids off the hook, but it communicates a powerful message: "I am for you not against you!"

"You Are CAPABLE (of wise behavior)"

The next message parents can communicate to their child is: "Even in your misbehavior I can see good things that God built into you. You are therefore capable of wiser behavior." Again, this is not what parents usually think of when they discipline. But let's face it, most misbehavior takes skill: skill God built into your child to be used for his purposes. When kids misbehave, parents typically dwell only on the bad, or sinful part of the action. As a result, the message typically communicated when we discipline, whether verbally or non-verbally, is: *"You are a problem!"*

When my child misbehaves for the umpteenth time in a day, it can be really hard to believe that he or she is capable of anything but making me crazy. But when I learn to prepare my heart and communicate love, it helps me to remember that with a little encouragement and guidance my child is quite capable of wise responses. I am inspired to see the skill beneath the sin and at least acknowledge it as a way of encouraging my child. Karla affirmed Nathan's skill and offered some reasonable choices to help him respond rationally.

- Karla affirmed Nathan saying, "Your persistence here is something God can use some day; it's just not helpful right now," and then "I can see you're really good at that game."

- She offered the choice, "If you pause the game immediately you can get back on again after your homework is done, but if not, then I'll decide how long it will be before you can play again."
- She set him up to succeed rather than focusing on his failure, but in a way that still kept him accountable for the behavior.

These kinds of responses, if respectfully delivered, open up whole new realms of possibilities for guiding our children through behavior challenges. Parents can learn to anchor their discipline in these principles: I prepare my heart and communicate to my child, "you are loved and you are capable." When they do, the discipline often connects with their child's heart and intercepts or redirects the misbehavior.

"You Are RESPONSIBLE (for your actions)"

In spite of our best efforts to follow these three principles, however, our children will still sometimes misbehave. When this happens, the Bible seems quite clear that we are commanded to use purposeful consequences in our discipline. The ultimate model for this discipline is God, who, we're told in Hebrews 12:10–11, "...disciplines us for our own good, that we may share in his holiness." This vision for disciplining in ways that lead our children into a deeper sense of God's holiness is what this book is really all about. So consequences, while they may indeed be painful (Heb 12:11) are not administered with the belief that enough pain will lead to change, but with the belief that growing and learning to get on the ramp of God's holiness can sometimes be painful. These consequences are delivered with love, not anger, as the primary mover.

Effective consequences communicate to our child, "*You* are responsible for your actions and for making amends when you've done something wrong." Proverbs 14:9 says, "Fools mock at making amends for sin, but goodwill is found among the upright." An important goal of discipline consequences is for our children to value the restitution that leads to reconciliation. In other words, what can I do when my kids mess up to help them feel remorse about what they've done (instead of angry at me for my controlling consequences), and to nurture a sincere desire to repent and make things right. Until I've achieved this goal, there's no telling how they will act when out from under my authority. The discipline used in this approach helps a child learn to take responsibility and not just "do time." Consequences, instead of being punitive, are constructive. Here are a few quick examples of constructive consequences:

- If a child disobediently goes on the computer before homework, he or she would be required to install a filter or timer, and teach the parent to use it.
- A child who disrespectfully yells at a sibling must sincerely write and say four things about the sibling that are encouraging and loving.
- A child who refuses to do clearly communicated household chores will not get social privileges until chores are complete.
- A child caught lying will help create a clear plan for what is needed to rebuild trust.

These are a few possibilities. Keep in mind that even the "right" consequence, imposed in a controlling or angry manner, will not ultimately produce the heart change parents are hoping for.

These ideas might seem unrealistic to parents for whom this kind of an approach to discipline is altogether foreign. That's what Dave thought one night when he came to a seminar on these principles, but he was desperate enough to try it because his nine-year-old son was spiraling out of control. His wife, Karen, called us several days later to say, "I can't believe the difference in my husband and how he deals with our son! How can I get more of your materials? We need to steep ourselves in these ideas."

We often see a cycle in families in which parents, worn out by discipline struggles, become more controlling and angry with their discipline. This leads to children feeling resentful and less likely to respond well to discipline efforts. Over time this cycle sets the tone of the relationship, which becomes characterized by anger and disconnection. Preventing this requires that parents learn to administer discipline gracefully.

Graceful administration is the core idea behind "Discipline that Connects." When children learn to expect grace in discipline, rather than power and control, their hearts become more open to their parents and ultimately more open to the redemptive power of the Gospel. Why? Because when grace is real in the context of discipline, children get a live demonstration of these critical Gospel truths:

- Though you have sinned, you are loved. Your sin cannot separate you from my love.
- You are capable and responsible to fulfill the purpose for which you were created.

When children experience these supportive and encouraging messages in the context of discipline, they begin to believe the messages. Children who believe these messages usually then learn to do the right things for the right reasons. They grow to be people who understand and grow in God's love, and learn to share that love with others.

Chapter 3

Forward Progress Begins with a Backward Step

One day I (Jim) came home stressed from work. The whole way home I was mulling over a contentious personnel issue at work, replaying the intense dialogue in my head. I pulled into the garage irritated, tired, and hungry. Oh how I longed for a straight and easy path to a quick snack and then my recliner.

When I opened the door I was greeted by all three of my children, who were gathered around the table arguing loudly and somewhat disrespectfully about a magazine. I dove right in. I grabbed the magazine and railed, "Would you kids be quiet! You're being rude and disrespectful. It's been a hard day and the last thing I need to come home to is your bickering."

The kids looked at me in shock, as if to ask, "Who's the rude one here?" But instead of railing right back, my eldest wisely commented, "Hey, Dad, where's the connection?"

Ouch!

"I'm sorry." I was sincere. "Could I have a do-over?"

This is a powerful example of how the Discipline that Connect principles have guided us not so much to get things right on the first try every time, but as a reminder to us when we have blown it. Once we have this reminder, grounded in the goals we have set for parenting, we can go back and rebuild, seeking to act on the goals in order to repair what our own misbehavior has broken.

When I asked for the "do-over" the kids nodded. I retreated to the garage. Behind the closed door, amidst the dust and clutter, I took a deep breath and whispered a short prayer, "Lord, forgive me. Help me to let go of my stuff from today. Help me to do better this time." I felt myself calm down and my attitude change as the Spirit of God brought me a bit of his peace and joy. I re-entered the house where the kids were waiting expectantly.

"Hey kids, great to see you!" I walked slowly over to them and sat down. "I see you're squabbling about that magazine. Do you want my help with it or can you respectfully work it out on your own?" I had now met my goals of preparing my heart and connecting well. I smiled. My confidence in them was high. And besides, my little "time-out" also bought them a little time to calm down. "We got it covered, Dad," my daughter offered. "Good do-over." They all smiled.

"Thanks to you too. And one other thing, if you're going to keep arguing I'd like you to take it downstairs or outside. I've had a stress-ful afternoon and need a little quiet time to recuperate." They quickly obeyed, even though their argument seemed finished anyway.

Since that day it has become clear to Lynne and me that almost all forward progress with our children begins by taking a step back to breathe, to pray, and to prepare our hearts and minds for the challenges before us. It's like a quarterback running his plays on the football field. He gets the ball and immediately takes a few steps back so that he can survey the field before making his next decision. Without those backward steps, he gets no separation from the chaos in front of him and can get quickly buried in it. Every once in a while he may strategically run a sneak where he gets the ball and dives into the pile hoping to gain a few inches. But if he did it on every play it would never work. He needs to consistently take a few steps back in order to make forward progress. Parenting is no different.

When I first came into the house that day, when I got the "ball" of my children's conflict, I just dove in like a quarterback sneak. I just lunged in with the weight of my stress and my agenda. No step back, no preparation, no surveying the "field" of what was going on with them and what was going on with me. I made no progress. In fact, I was thrown for a loss. Only by stepping back could I prepare. In that brief step back into my garage I realized that it needed to be just God and me before I engaged with my family. That short time to prepare my heart by praying and taking a few deep breaths made all the difference.

The Long-term Impact of Charging into Discipline

Parents often describe their transition to the teenage years this way: "We had a few bumps here and there when our child was young, but things have been pretty much under control. But lately it's like overnight the lid just came off. What happened? I don't even know this kid!" The following story could help answer that question. It's a fictional composite of things teens have expressed to us in our 25 years of ministry with struggling families. It's an example of the way parents use consequences with no thought beyond gaining immediate control. It's also a story about what kids learn when this happens.

"You're so old-fashioned. This is stupid!" Twelve-year-old Kayla screamed at her dad, Joe, who had just grounded Kayla for defying instructions to clean the kitchen before using the computer.

"How dare you talk to me that way!" Joe was stern, taking a dominant posture and adding consequences as the conflict escalated. "You go to your room! And if you expect to ever wear that jacket again you apologize right now." Joe's frustration was boiling over. He couldn't figure out what had come over Kayla in recent weeks as her behavior grew increasingly irrational and defiant. This was going to be the last straw.

Kayla felt trapped. She didn't feel the least bit sorry, but she didn't want to lose the expensive jacket her mom had bought as her birthday gift. Exasperated with her dad's power-hungry tactics and confused about what her jacket had to do with any of this, Kayla ultimately felt defeated. Not able to put words to her feelings and knowing better than to lash out for fear of losing her jacket, she gave in. "I'm sorry!" she forced, and loudly shut the door to her room. The consequences had worked, if working meant getting Kayla to say the words "I'm sorry."

Joe huffed and went back to his business, feeling satisfied that Kayla had learned her lesson, but still worried about how difficult it was becoming to keep her in line. "After all," he thought, "I'm just doing what I've always done and she's getting worse." He prayed that God would convict Kayla of her attitude and that she would somehow get over this season of rebellion she was in. Beneath this prayer were feelings he did not yet understand or have words to express. But Joe avoided looking at his own heart and responses in the conflict. He had a deep fear about where this was all leading so the focus of his thoughts remained on Kayla.

In the relative safety of her room, Kayla's rage gave way to sobs. Any potential for remorse was trampled by confusion, hurt, rage, and powerlessness. She totally blamed her dad for how lousy she felt. As these thoughts and feelings boiled, Kayla grew determined to not give in so easily next time.

As a budding adolescent, Kayla was beginning to feel more able to take her parents on and win. "He better not mess me over again," Kayla thought, "or he'll be sorry. I'm not backin' down next time. I don't care if he freaks out. They can't keep pushing me around like they have all my life." She took comfort in her plan and drifted off to sleep.

This story is fairly typical of the stories we hear from families we've worked with, as well as the reports we hear from adolescents about how they experience their parents' discipline. Is it any wonder why "the lid comes off" so often as kids reach early teen years? The pent-up feelings from being exasperated by well-meaning but misguided discipline tends to come out in all kinds of ugly ways if parents don't give thought to more than just immediate control.

We can get away with exasperating our children with unfair or harsh consequences when they are young. The children are enough afraid of us that they will do what we ask of them not because they respect us, or really want to do what's right, but because they're afraid. We are simply

> Kids' pent-up feelings from being exasperated by well-meaning but misguided discipline tends to come out in all kinds of ugly ways if parents don't give thought to more than just immediate control.

more powerful, and they know (most of them) that they will get "put in their place" if they challenge us. So they don't mess with us until they figure out how powerful they can be.

This puts the apostle Paul's teaching to parents in Ephesians 6:4 in a whole new light. "...do not exasperate your children; instead, bring them up in the training and instruction of the Lord."

I (Jim) once interviewed some teens about this. I asked, "Do you think, when you misbehave, that your parents ever misbehave too in the way they react to you?" Without hesitation the first teen answered, "They sure do!" and he quickly added, "but there is no one to hold them accountable for it." Another teen added, "Since there's no one to hold them accountable for it, I have to get even with them, so I do whatever I have to do to get them pissed!" Her strategy was clear—when her parents were harsh and punitive, she was harsh and vengeful.

This kind of thing can happen with younger children too. We watched this scene unfold with a mom and her toddler. Kirsten firmly announced that it was time to leave. Two-year-old Owen shook his head as she swept in to grab his hand to go. He defiantly yelled "No," dodged her hand and then took a swing to hit her. Kirsten bristled. She was stuck in a common parenting dilemma, feeling caught somewhere between her child's disobedience and disrespect and her own fear, embarrassment, and selfish desire to be in control.

She reacted loudly, "You may not say 'no' to me and hit me." She picked him up like a rag doll and plopped him on his time-out chair.

Owen stomped his feet and flailed his arms screaming, "No! No! No!"

She continued yelling, her nose just inches from his, "Now you stay in that time-out chair and don't move until the timer goes off. Do you understand me?"

"NO!" her son screamed and stood up from the chair.

Indeed he did not understand her. Truth be told, she did not understand herself either. In her confusion she did what she had learned from her mother; namely, to act angry in hopes of gaining control. When parents get irate like this, and in their anger yell instructions in order to gain a sense of control, children lose the ability to process words and thoughts. The child learns not from the words being spoken but from the actions being shown. They demonstrate this learning by imitating or "mirroring" their parents. Whatever the parent feels and expresses is likely to be what the child feels and expresses in return.

In this mother-and-son power struggle, the "mirror" dynamic

played out further. Kirsten ran out of tactics as their conflict continued. Feeling overwhelmed and lost about what to do next, she burst into tears of desperation and stormed off saying, "I don't need this right now." When she transitioned from anger to despair, her son imitated again. Where seconds before he was postured to angrily run from the time-out chair as he imitated her anger, he now sat down in the chair and sobbed big, sad tears. His defiant energy was deflated as he wailed, "Mommy!" (deep breath) "Mommy!"

The challenges of parenting are relentless. At any moment these little people's persistent, creative, and selfish misbehavior can trigger impulsive, irrational responses in a normally quite rational adult. When parents get loud, unpredictable, and intimidating, children feel threatened. Kids who are afraid (just like grown-ups) often fight back, or they may be intimidated into compliance. But either way, these kids are not thinking about learning from their mistakes. They are just protecting themselves against their parents by either imitating to fight back, or backing down in order to stay out of trouble. The learning is not about respect and obedience, but about control and avoidance.

Parents will act this way as long as it "works" for them. By that we mean that it gains the parent an immediate sense of control. Over time, however, this approach becomes less effective as children's mistrust or resentment of their parent builds and the children grow more physically and mentally able to fight back. When the angry approach quits working for parents, they tend to either ramp up their efforts and escalate conflicts, fueled by resentment of their children, or they become more passive to avoid the conflicts, leaving the kids to increasingly "run the show."

These two opposite responses of "give in" or "blow up" can actually feed each other. Give-in parents get exasperated as they succumb to increasing demands from their small tyrant until they've had it and suddenly lash out. Blow-up parents become fearful of the escalating tension and begin to give in to their child's demands just to keep the peace.

Even if the situation doesn't escalate to become that extreme, there are subtle but important messages communicated by impulsive, emotional discipline methods. In Matthew 12:34, Jesus said, "… out of the overflow of the heart the mouth speaks." When a parent's overflow is out of a heart of anger, anxiety, or need to control, the messages children perceive from parents might be:

- "I am out to get you"
- "You are a problem"
- "You make me angry" (which puts the child in control of the parent's emotions)
- "I don't really love you when you act this way"

When children perceive these messages they most likely will resist our efforts. Even if they are compliant to avoid rejection or punishment, rarely do they build the values that motivate them to want to do the right thing for good reasons.

The early years in the Jackson household were characterized by irritable, impulsive, sensory-sensitive kids and stressed-out, reactive parents. Daniel, our strong-willed oldest, used to say to Lynne, "Mom, you just bursted all over us." He and Jim would lock in "alpha male" power struggles with intense emotions. The conflict level in our home was part of the reason that Jim's sister sadly observed, "You guys are the most stressed family I know." We were the most stressed family we knew, too, and we were desperate to find a better way to parent. Learning to prepare our hearts was a critical starting point.

Chapter 4

The Safety of a Prepared Heart

After hearing about the importance of preparing hearts to discipline, a parent once remarked, "Oh, I get it, that's how to protect my kids from my baggage." This was a great analogy for the importance of preparing our hearts for discipline. We all have baggage. Some of us more than others. The following somewhat extreme example illustrates how that baggage can complicate our discipline efforts, and how one parent started taking responsibility to prepare her heart and protect her kids from her baggage.

Linda was a single mom who had left an abusive husband. Her parents had been dominant and controlling. So she naturally gravitated toward and married a man who was dominant and controlling because that was what felt familiar and predictable to her. As he became physically abusive to her she feared for her life. She left her husband after church-led attempts to support and counsel them failed, and a restraining order was needed to keep the kids safe from his abusive threats. This was her baggage. But she refused to let it define her.

As Linda embarked on a healing journey of counseling, prayer, and rebuilding her community, she could see how her baggage frequently spilled over into her parenting. Resentment about her childhood, her ex-husband, and fear that her kids could turn out like him surfaced whenever the kids were disobedient or defiant. Knowing it was not helpful to allow that baggage to compel her discipline, she made a goal to calm down before dealing with the boys' frequent misbehavior. One exhausting day, she heard her boys escalating into an intense conflict over a demolished Lego creation. "You wrecked it!""I did not!" The third one chimed in, "I saw you step on it!"

Linda charged in. She intended to strongly reprimand the careless child and the others who were ready to aggressively deliver "justice." But she realized that her baggage-laden approach would likely (as it had before) fuel her kids' anger toward one another. She caught herself, and instead screeched to a halt and began counting loudly to ten. Her boys stared at her with "What's-up-with-Mom?" shock. Still angry, she counted again, slowing down and relaxing some. She still needed one more ten count to fully settle down. By the end of her third repetition of ten, she was able to smile. The boys started to giggle and then they all burst out in laughter. With the tension about the problem gone, Linda was able to guide the boys through a constructive resolution. But more important than that, she had modeled how to make a wise choice to calm down when really upset. And, like most kids, her boys were watching their parent's example. The next day she heard her middle son coaching her youngest who was revving up for a good tantrum, "Don't get mad. Remember, count to ten." We could all bear to follow Linda's example. Regardless of what baggage we carry into conflict, this approach can protect our kids from it.

Indeed we all have baggage: stress from the day, fear about where this misbehavior will lead if it continues, resentment that our child hasn't appreciated us, or leftover issues from our past. Even the way we were parented is part of our "baggage." When our baggage fuels our discipline, we lay a heavy burden on our children to behave not just for their own benefit, but for ours.

But when I take the backward step to consider "What's going on under the surface with me and how can I calm myself down?" I protect my children from things that have nothing to do with their misbehavior; from my "baggage." I prepare my heart.

When this happens, I feel much safer to my child. The messages my child perceives are altogether different. My child hears:

- "I am for you"
- "I love you no matter what"
- "You are capable of getting through this and resolving it"
- "You are responsible and, even if your consequence is hard for you, I am here"

Are these not the messages God demonstrates for us? When we can discipline in ways that communicate these messages, our children will open their hearts to our influence. But more important than that, they become open to the very message of the Gospel.

The Power of a Parent's Example

Neither parents nor their kids learn much when they are stressed and upset. When parents are upset, kids get upset too and tend to focus on Mom's or Dad's anger or stress instead of on their own misbehavior. For example, if Mom yells angrily at Aidan for picking on his little sister, Sandra, Aidan is likely to focus on how mean and unfair Mom is and how much she favors Sandra. He may even be plot-

> Children are much more likely to take responsibility for their behavior if parents are responsible for their own behavior first.

ing how he's gonna get back at Sandra when Mom's not looking.

Children are much more likely to take responsibility for their behavior if parents are responsible for their own behavior first. Just like adults, children will almost always deny their own misbehavior, if they feel unsafe or "attacked" in any way. If Mom prepares her heart first, she will be calm and able to think of ways to help Aidan consider how his behavior was unkind to Sandra. She can then help him figure out a better way to respond, thus nurturing in him a desire to respond in a better way next time.

A calm, prepared heart is the starting place to help children want to behave appropriately for the right reasons, not just to avoid a parent's wrath. Thoughtful parents can connect with their child about the below-the-surface thoughts and feelings such as hurt, frustration, anxiety, or anger that often drive the misbehavior in the first place.

Kid's "Mirror" Their Parent's Feelings and Actions

God has created our brains with important cells called mirror cells. These cells cause us to experience what we see happening to other people. They might cause us to stand on our tiptoes when we watch a high jumper, or nod when the person talking to us nods. Mirror cells spark empathy when we listen to someone share something deeply emotional. And, they are the cells responsible for why children learn so much from watching their parents. It's what caused Owen on the time-out chair to mirror the escalating emotions of his mother. But when parents prepare their hearts before discipline, they help their child mirror and practice a really important life skill—how to calm down and think clearly in stressful situations.

It's usually an exercise in frustration for a parent to simply self-lecture: "I've got to be more patient." It is a much more inspiring goal to disciple my child in how to patiently handle stress and conflict. I do this as I act on the belief that Jesus is present and merciful even in messy family conflicts. He gives me self-control and clear thinking to solve the problem. Imagine how my children's future marriages, ministries, and work experiences might be strengthened if they learn to effectively, prayerfully prepare their hearts before engaging in challenging interactions. Even if I have no clue what to do in response to my child's difficult behavior, if I model taking a break to think about it, I've accomplished a lot.

"Thinking Out loud" Gives Insight

Children learn even more effectively from our example if we talk out loud about our process—describing our feelings and our strategy to calm down. Daniel and I (Lynne) still butted heads with some intensity when he was a teenager. I'd point my finger at him after some disrespectful, sarcastic blast. "You can't talk to me that way!" I'd say strongly, with as much authority as I could muster. But of course he could talk to me that way anytime he chose. So my authority was rendered rather meaningless as I proclaimed what we both knew was not true.

We started to resolve things much more quickly when I learned instead to say, "Daniel, I'm feeling really angry right now, and I'm afraid I'm going to be disrespectful to you, so I want to take a break. Let's finish this conversation when we are both calmer." Just this goal of keeping my own head cool and explaining my thinking to Daniel was a healing balm in our relationship. Before long Daniel started following my lead. The change took place over years, but now as a young adult he almost always keeps a very cool head in conflict.

This is helpful with children as young as two. Owen is a sensitive little kid who detects any under-the-surface anxiety in his mom, Kirsten. He reacts to the subtle changes in how she responds to him, and starts to act up. Fortunately for both of them, Kirsten has learned that when she is calm, so is Owen. She has made huge strides in staying calm and peaceful since the incident on the time-out chair. Just recently, when stressed about an upcoming trip, the two of them were mirroring each other's anxiety and starting to wind up in a power struggle. She realized what was happening, picked Owen up and said gently, "Owen, Mommy's really stressed. I know that stresses you too. Let's calm down together." They snuggled briefly and finished the evening joyful and connected.

Thinking out loud accomplishes two important things. First, as in the experiences of Daniel and Owen, it becomes an example for our children. When they hear how we think our way through things, they can learn from it. If we keep our thoughts to ourselves, they probably won't figure out and learn from why we responded as we did. I (Lynne) stayed calmer in response to my kids' whining if I stated, "If I give you what you want when you whine, that teaches you that whining is a good way to get what you want, and that's not true. Maybe later, when you're calm, we can talk about it." It was better for the kids and for me than if I had just said, "Your whining is not OK, so stop it!"

The second thing is that thinking out loud holds parents accountable to better thinking. We've asked many parents about what concrete thoughts they think when they face challenges with their kids. Most cannot answer. When asked about what their thoughts and feelings were when they disciplined, parents will often say, "I'm just trying to get him to do the right thing," or, "I'm trying to teach her some respect." But when asked, "What specific thoughts and feelings were going on inside you at the time?" many parents can't answer.

When we are forced to think out loud, it forces us to identify our feelings, as Lynne did when she said, "I'm feeling angry." It forces us to name our goal: "I don't want to disrespect you," or, "I want to be sure you feel loved, even though I'm going to talk about your behavior," or, "I want to affirm the good part of what you did before dealing with your misbehavior." This kind of process tends to disarm both parent and child. It helps to keep the interaction calmer and more constructive.

Wise Use of Scripture

The Holy Scriptures provide tremendous wisdom for discipline. But it requires great discernment to be maturely guided by those principles. All too often we see and hear angry parents use the Bible to shame kids. It leaves a sour taste in children's spirits for what they perceive is a "policeman in the sky" kind of God who is usually displeased with them.

For example, when a child misbehaves a parent might angrily announce, "Even if I didn't see it, Jesus was watching!" Or if a child mistreats a sibling a parent might even quote scripture, (drawing from Eph. 4:32), "The Bible says, 'Be kind and compassionate to one another,' and that was not kind!" These are clearly not statements about God's grace and truth that will be attractive to our children. Kids who usually hear the Bible used to correct their misbehavior are almost certain to develop distaste for it.

Referencing and applying scriptural teaching wisely requires parents to thoughtfully prepare their own hearts and consider the example they set for the value of God's Word. As a parent, do you value the liberating and grace-filled message of the Gospel? Do you gain encouragement from God's word, and guidance through your own struggle with sin? If so, do you speak with your kids about the wisdom and joy of obedience? Your example is the starting place for teaching children to love the reproof of God's Word.

Once you're working on setting this example, it takes great discernment *and* a calm spirit to use scripture well in discipline situations. If you're ticked off – best to wait! Stop and consider, "Would my use of scripture wound or woo my child right now?"

Scripture can come to life when God activates a verse or principle from his Word in your own life during a conflict with your child. It might be a prompting to stay peaceful or to ask forgiveness. It might be a principle you learned or that shaped you, which you then discuss with your child. When you model how you apply the verse you want your kids to learn, *then* you will have credibility to proactively teach and encourage your children. The following real-life example deepened the way we think about this.

On one occasion, Daniel and I (Lynne) had been strongly butting heads all morning. He suggested we go play tennis to reconnect after the conflict. On the court I was still sour and was taking out my residual anger at him on the poor tennis ball. When I angrily smashed a shot into the net Daniel quizzically asked, "Mom are you still mad?" In that instant I was reminded of some verses I'd been studying, and felt convicted by the command in Philippians 4:8 to focus on anything worthy of praise. So I approached the net and said, "Daniel, I've been focusing on what you did wrong. But just now the Lord convicted me that I didn't notice you did something really cool—you wanted to reconnect by having fun together after we were mad." I shared the whole verse with him and his face lit up, "I love that verse!" God's work in me spilled over to my son, and since then he has been drawn to that verse many times in difficult interactions with others.

We All Grow in God's Love and Grace

As I commit to seek God for the love and grace my misbehaving child needs, I am constantly reminded of the truth that "out of the abundance of my heart my mouth speaks" (Matt. 12:34). If I am at a place of feeling loved that love flows quite freely. If I have been graced, then grace flows. If not, well, then I find it hard to sincerely say graceful and loving words or commit graceful, loving acts.

Let's admit it; we've all got baggage. We have not been perfectly graced and loved. Whether it was today, last week, last month, last year, or throughout our lives, almost everyone has leftover pain or bitterness because we have been raised and surrounded by imperfect people. Understanding this, and growing in my ability to receive grace from God and from people prepares me to better demonstrate God's grace to my children.

Perhaps more than anything in life, our three kids have driven Lynne and me to the Scriptures to learn and grow in the Perfect Lover's love for us, to know his peace that surpasses understanding and to receive the truth that there is no condemnation to those who are in Christ Jesus. We still have much to learn, but our fight of faith is to believe and walk in this truth for parenting: My value is not based on how or what my kids do; it is based on what Jesus did in the ultimate act of love for me at the cross.

The most important work I can do as a parent is to grasp how wide and high and long and deep is the love of Christ for me. The more I believe, the more I receive the Peace, Love, and Grace of Christ. The more I receive, the more I pass it on to my children. This is at the core of my work to prepare my heart for discipline.

Chapter 5

The Nuts and Bolts of Becoming a Calmer Parent

Eight-year-old Ethan accidentally threw the Nerf football into a crowd of guests at the outdoor gathering, hitting one of them on the forehead. His mom, Ellen, was a little uncomfortable in this gathering of people she barely knew. She popped out of the crowd and immediately scolded Ethan for his carelessness and his disrespect of the guests. She then told him to go inside and take a time out. He was clearly upset and ashamed.

What Ellen missed in this was that Ethan was not aiming at the crowd. He was obviously a novice at throwing a Nerf and it stayed in his hand much longer than he anticipated as he tried to launch it over a small tree. It was a fairly safe intention. But Ellen, obviously embarrassed and angered, acted quickly to punish Ethan. She did nothing to find out from Ethan what had happened, how he might have done it differently, and what he could do to make amends to the person he'd hit. In this incident Ellen missed a great opportunity to address Ethan's poor judgment in a way that would encourage him rather than discourage.

While most misbehavior does not demand immediate intervention, parents often feel an immediate need to intervene anyway. They tend to jump into situations with a sense of urgency, try to control things and then justify their actions "because of my child's misbehavior." This is rarely helpful, because discipline interactions flow from a complex combination of what's going on with the child and what's going on inside the parent. Preparing my heart helps me do the spiritual and mental work needed to understand my part in it and more effectively address what's going on in my child.

So let's get practical about how to slow down and prepare our hearts. We've developed a little phrase based on our quarterback analogy—"Step back. Get perspective."

"Step Back. Get Perspective."

Step back. When you feel yourself charging into a conflict, stop (unless someone's safety is at risk, of course) and notice what's physically going on in you. You may feel ears burning, a knot in the stomach, a clenched jaw, a change in your tone of voice, muscle tension, or intimidating body language. These physical symptoms of stress are the first clue that there is more going on inside of you. There are thoughts and feelings stirring that serve as the fuel for these physical responses. As you get in touch with these symptoms, you realize that the difficult interactions typical of discipline situations are not just because a child misbehaved.

> Preparing my heart helps me understand my part, and more effectively address what's going on in my child.

The "Step back" part of this phrase has helped Lynne and me many times. One particular time I (Jim) watched my kids get into an argument. As the disrespectful banter began flying I was tempted to jump in. I could feel my ears getting red, the first obvious sign that I'm getting peeved. As I inhaled to unleash my angry reaction on my kids, I recognized the impulse and stopped dead in my tracks. There was no hurry here. No one was in danger. So I waited in the shadows to see how it would unfold.

Within a few minutes (longer than I would have liked but

pretty good for kids their age, or any age) they had apologized, worked it out and happily continued chatting. Instead of hearing from me how rude and disrespectful they were, and getting some unhelpful consequence for their sins, they instead learned that they could resolve conflicts on their own and that apologizing is sometimes the best way to get there. Hmmmm. Which outcome seems most preferable? That's right, the one where an angry dad stops and lets his kids figure it out for themselves.

Once you've stopped the charge, you can calm yourself physically; i.e., moving back to a calmer state. Since "motion changes emotion," your body can help your brain function better and access the skills you need to deal with the challenge. Some practical ideas to calm down that have worked for parents we've coached are:

- Physically take a step back instead of forward.
- Instead of towering over your child, sit down next to him or her. Or sit down, lean back and put your feet up.
- Walk slowly instead of rapidly toward the situation.
- Go to a different room for a few minutes and let your child know you're going to cool down a bit before trying to resolve the conflict.
- Breathe deeply and slowly. Breathing deeply releases endorphins and changes the brain chemistry with which you engage a misbehaving child.

Doing things like this to get space and buy time definitely help a parent calm down and respond more wisely. In working with explosive, at-risk youth, as long as a discipline situation/conflict was safe, I (Jim) was trained to make my first goal buying some time. Many parents have found that simple "buy time" statements are extremely effective. For example, "There needs to be a consequence for this, but I'm going to take some time to consider what's best." This also gives a child a chance to think about what he's done.

We know a day-care provider who carries a small bottle of hand lotion in her pocket. "I take the child aside, but I don't say a word about the misbehavior until I've put lotion on my hands and finished rubbing it in. By then I've usually calmed down and have come up with a plan to deal with the situation wisely." Once parents discover and practice the best ways to calm down, they can get perspective on what's going on.

Get Perspective. This is truly as simple as asking yourself the question, "What's going on in me – What am I thinking and feeling? How will that affect my child?" At the deepest level, these brave questions invite us to be deeply introspective before God and his word. But in the heat of the moment, they at least help us to develop more helpful ways of interpreting and dealing with what's happening. Here are a few strategies for growing in perspective that we've learned from other parents over the years:

- Prayer—i.e., "God, give me wisdom. Help me forgive. Give me your heart for my child."
- Recite a scripture. One mom's favorite verse for parenting stress is Matthew 25:40, "Whatever you did for one of the least of these… you did for Me." When she was really upset, she'd say it out loud, which also seemed to calm her child.
- To keep from blowing the incident out of proportion, remember something you love about your child, or a recent fond memory. This can be difficult to think about when you're up-

set, so plan ahead: What is a favorite memory of your child being respectful, thoughtful, obedient, etc.? One wise dad simply reminds himself, "Ah, I love this kid."

- Consciously walk in your child's shoes. What is he or she feeling? Have you ever felt similar emotions? What does your child need right now?

- Prepare to make the most of a difficult situation by considering, "What's the opportunity here?" i.e., how can I connect or build life skills through this situation? This was the phrase that most helped me (Lynne) respond peacefully and purposely when things got tough.

All this may sound a bit lofty, but it can be so practical and helpful. I (Lynne) had a defining moment one day when locked in an angry, nose-to-nose conflict with Daniel. We were stuck in our classic roles: He was ticked off about something and I was determined to stop his tirade. I felt the weight of my discouragement becoming oppressive as we escalated but, as I stopped to get some different perspective, I suddenly became aware of God's loving presence in the midst of our mess. I knew that he had compassion on how hard it was for our two intense personalities to get along peacefully. I looked Daniel in the eye and said softly, "You know what I'm thinking right now?" He looked puzzled. I continued, "God has so much mercy on us in our struggle."

Just this acknowledgment settled us both. We calmed down and worked through our conflict respectfully. It strengthened our relationship. This was years ago, but the memory is still vivid for me, and I've returned to the truth of God's mercy and presence during numerous other messy moments.

Changing Habits When I Feel Stuck

If you realize you've started a discipline interaction with an explosion, re-group as quickly as possible. This allows you to practice and strengthen the kind of response you really want to make, even after getting off to a rough start. The more you practice regrouping, the quicker that ability to regroup will come and the more common it will be to start with a calmer approach. And, your kids just might learn something from you.

Lana was struggling with Mike, her 11-year-old, who was frustrated by some learning challenges. He hated being behind most of his peers in school. Lana and Mike seemed to butt heads quickly, especially over responsibilities or homework. When Lana heard the "Discipline that Connects" principles, she began to work on self-calming and regrouping with a "do-over" if she started to get upset. One day Mike started to escalate during a conflict about his math homework, but then he stopped suddenly and said, "Mom, can I have a do-over?" Lana realized the value of the self-awareness and humility she had modeled for her child. Over time, staying cool in conflict became easier for both of them.

Another helpful way to grow in this "staying-cool-in-conflict" approach is to focus on whatever went well in your effort to stay calmer in response to misbehavior, even if it was just to lower your tone of voice slightly before an otherwise impulsive reaction. Your focus on and satisfaction with your success will grow more success. Make a mental note, tell someone else, or simply thank God for his grace when you remember to discipline peacefully. But no matter what, rest in the grace and encouragement of Jesus that is there for you. Remember, this is a small-steps process with lots of ups and downs, but it has big pay-offs in the long run.

Jeri and I (Lynne) had several coaching sessions where part of the time was focused on how to stay calm when her anxious, intense, and sensitive daughter would have a meltdown. Jeri was particularly discouraged at her angry response when her daughter started screaming about the texture of the towel under her booster seat in the car. Nearly in tears, Jeri said, "I feel so guilty for yelling at her like that." With further questioning, she admitted, "Well, it wasn't pretty, but I guess I didn't lose it completely." I challenged her to put her focus on whatever success she had at learning to stay calm. Her daughter was still struggling. Even the sensation of getting her fingernails clipped could send the poor girl into a meltdown, but Jeri was learning to stay calm when the chaos happened. A few months later she emailed a review of progress: "I'm amazingly calm most of the time."

The bottom line when things don't go well is to hang on to a faith-filled perspective: God is at work for his good purposes. Jim and I struggled greatly in learning how to be peaceful in discipline. Jim often had quick-tempered reactions and I struggled with a rigid perfectionism that made me hard on the kids and hard on myself. The whole family had to be happy and respectful before I could feel good and, of course, that was rare. My anger would often slowly rise through the day along with my discouragement. I have painful memories from those days. On two separate occasions I whacked a child across the face in my exasperation. There were many times when I lamented that I was getting nowhere in the journey of becoming a more peaceful, loving parent.

At one particularly low point I felt absolutely stuck in my critical perfectionism and figured it was useless to keep trying to change it. I believe the Lord gave me the insight that I needed: My children will have persistent life-long struggles too. What do I want to model for them—despair and defeat, or faith and persistence? That thought gave me the courage to keep pursuing God's peace and love in the chaos, with gradual but strong changes over the years. Jim and I are still growing in this and we are in our 50s.

The fruit of that persistence helped me encourage our daughter recently about her chronic struggle with disorganization. We'd had numerous discussions before about helpful strategies, but this time was different. She was ready to give up trying. I shared how I had felt hopeless and ready to give up in the battle against my critical perfectionism, and she saw in me first-hand the fruits of faith and perseverance in chronic challenges. Our conversation became encouraging and fruitful.

Chapter 6

Renewing My Mind for Parenting

Many parents come to us lamenting that they feel stuck in unhealthy patterns. Despite their best efforts and resolutions, nothing changes, and conflict often sets the tone in their families. As we explore further it usually becomes clear that their efforts are about changing surface behavior without changing the thinking that drives it. The Bible tells us in Romans 12:2 "Do not conform any longer to the pattern of this world, but be transformed by the renewing of your mind." As it relates to parenting, the pattern of this world is to deal with things on the surface. If our children persist in bad behavior, we blame them. We try new techniques to modify their behaviors, but the methods typically don't work well because our children react to our underlying anxiety and stress. Then the cycle repeats itself.

Being transformed is about deep change. The renewing of our minds is about thinking new thoughts and new attitudes. In order to have these changed, we have to know what they are and how they impact our parenting. We have to dig beneath the surface and allow God to search our hearts.

"I've gotta look below the surface if I want to grow as a parent"

If a little leaven really does leaven the whole loaf (i.e., the whole family), then it's quite possible the reason our kids keep acting up is that we are harboring the leaven of resentment or fear or unhelpful and untrue thoughts about our children. Maybe we have not taken responsibility for our own transformation and renewal. A persistent discipline challenge just may be a gift from God to help parents get their focus off of their child's behavior, and onto their own transformation. In other words, the only way real growth can happen is when parents focus on their own transformation. And if our children are going to be transformed someday by the renewing of their minds, we are their primary example for this.

So if I really want to grow as a parent, I have to be willing to look inside my own thoughts, feelings, and motives and then surrender them to God's grace and truth. Behavior challenges with my children give me, perhaps, my best opportunity to say out loud the thoughts that drive me and submit them to God for transformation by the renewal of my mind.

> The challenges of parenting hold a mirror for me to see what's really in my heart.

The challenges of parenting hold a mirror for me to see what's really in my heart. The strong emotions, actions, and statements revealed when I discipline are an indication that there's a lot going on under the surface. The thoughts or beliefs that cause strong emotions and reactions to kids' misbehavior come in an endless variety, but the following are some typical, persistent thoughts that parents have identified.

"You should obey because I'm the parent"

I (Jim) needed my mind renewed about a persistent problem with my firstborn. I grew up in a home where arguing with Dad was absolutely taboo. As a result, I had these rules about arguing embedded in my mind: "It is not okay to argue with Dad. Dad is right because Dad says…"

When Daniel started arguing with me, I was unaware that I was operating by my own father's rules. I simply got irritated when he challenged me and judged that he should know better. As far as I was concerned he was the problem for being argumentative, and I frequently found myself saying and believing that he should stop arguing "because I am your dad, and I said so!"

But Daniel was less fearful of me than I was of my dad. So even when I said "No," he persisted. It wasn't that he wanted to defy me; it was that he really wanted to understand my rationale for things. The answer, "because Dad says" did not satisfy his need to have concepts make sense. So he continued to challenge me. I tried to find new parenting strategies and consequences to get him to stop arguing, but as long as I had the unexamined "because I said" rules floating around in my brain, and he had a need to know in his mind, nothing I tried was effective. Then, when Daniel was a young teen, we had our defining moment relative to this dynamic. After again arguing longer than I cared to, I flat out said to Daniel, "I know you don't like it, but I'm the dad! You need to stop this right now because I don't want to be frustrated about this anymore!"

It's interesting how, when we say out loud the thoughts and feelings that drive us, they sometimes sound so ridiculous. Essentially I had just admitted that the reason I was saying "no" was because of my frustration. It had nothing at all to do with what was best for Daniel. What he said next will be forever etched in my brain. "Dad, I want to respect you. And I'll be quiet if you want. But if soothing your frustration is the best reason you can give, it will be very hard for me to respect you the way I want to respect you."

What penetrating depth his statement bore. *"I want to respect you!"* It forced me to look inward and ask myself a few questions, "Why am I being so demanding right now? Why do I so need to make him stop arguing when he wants so badly to really understand? What does my frustration have to do with anything? What makes me think that I even have sound rationale for demanding that he stop?" I also wondered if his statement wasn't the heart cry of many children who appear contentious or disrespectful. At the core of the matter, kids *want to respect* their parents, but parents don't do the hard work of earning the respect.

I realized, even after years of working on being a more respectful and godly parent, that I was addressing my son's argumentativeness according to the same rules implanted in my brain as a youngster. "I'm the dad...because I said." This was a hard pill for me to swallow. I had to confess that as a person still inclined to sinful motives, the reason "because I said" or "because I'm frustrated" was not a very solid rationale for forcing my children to comply. I confessed to him that my demands were rooted in selfishness and that I wanted to do a better job of letting God shape new thoughts to guide me better when we argued.

This is how God "transforms us by the renewing of our minds." He confronts us with our worldly thinking. Then, through the truth of the Scriptures, he speaks truth to our minds. What happened with Daniel and me was that through my out-loud statement, my worldly thinking was exposed. Then, as I took this issue to God in prayer, I began to develop a new set of beliefs about Daniel's arguing and test them against the truth of God's word. Here are a few of the renewed mind thoughts that God shaped in me:

- Daniel misbehaved. But in my effort to make it stop, I misbehaved too. When I am accountable for my misbehavior, I win his respect.
- For my "no" to be respected, I must have a sound rationale for it.

- Sometimes I'm wrong. So I'd better be careful about demanding that my children comply when I'm wrong.
- Daniel is miraculously created to question and solve things. I can either force him to comply and build resentment in him or find ways to draw out that miracle.
- There are times when I will demand immediate obedience because I truly believe it to be best. When those times come, true, heartfelt obedience will result if I have proved myself respectful and trustworthy.

This does not mean that every child should be allowed to argue every time a request is made. But we have found that when parents are accountable for stating a reasonable rationale for their requests, it helps them grow to be more reasonable, and it helps the kids understand. When they understand, they are more likely to respect and obey the requests—even those rare requests that come without explanation. We knew this was a helpful process for Daniel because as we helped him understand the reasons for our requests, he grew increasingly obedient. He really did want to understand and grow and this was his way of wrestling with our values.

"My child is a real problem! I have fear about where this will lead him."

When parents see their child struggling with behavioral problems, it can cause strong anxiety which surfaces as anger. Parents may view it as a character flaw, wonder if they are to blame and worry what will happen to their child. I (Lynne) had to do some digging to understand and work through that kind of thought pattern.

My early parenting experience was filled with stressful conflicts and dark thoughts. These thoughts were sometimes like a loop tape that kept playing over and over in my head, especially when I would butt heads with our oldest son, Daniel. He made me feel like a failure as a mother, and I felt so guilty about how much I resented him. My most memorable unhelpful belief was, "I'm an angry mom, raising an angry child; when he gets to be a teenager, it's gonna be horrible." This anxious thinking fueled my frequent discouragement and angry responses. It also made me more determined to control his behavior immediately so the "terrible teenager" scenario I feared wouldn't happen.

The Holy Spirit began to confront me about the way I was not "speaking the truth in love" (see Ephesians 4:15) to myself. I realized I needed to develop a different loop tape to substitute for that thought. After some prayer and thoughtfulness, I finally landed on, "I'm an intense mom raising an intense child and we butt heads, but we love each other." I consciously practiced that thought as Daniel and I started into a conflict, and it helped me to choose a calmer response. Over time, as I learned to look at the big picture of my relationship with him through the lenses of faith and hope, I developed a new belief that raising this child was a hilarious adventure. He grew to be a teenager with strong character, a passionate follower of Jesus—intense, witty, occasionally exasperating, but very endearing. By the grace of God he was nothing like what I had dreaded.

After hearing this story, Brad realized he had an anxious judgment for a loop tape when his 11-year-old daughter started to melt down. He emailed us the details of his story.

"Sarah's defiance and outbursts used to upset me a lot, and I viewed her as a relational 'train wreck.' The Lord convicted me of this critical attitude which was hurting my relationship with her.

"I have since learned to shift my thinking away from fixating on this negative perspective to seeing her for what she truly is. She is a stunningly creative, passionate, and gifted person who passionately loves God and other people. For Sarah, life is an opportunity to put the 'pedal to the metal' and just go for it. And when she goes for it, the results are beautiful. I am so thankful that I've begun to see her more as God sees her. She is not a train wreck; she's a masterpiece. The transformation in our relationship has been dramatic."

Parents sometimes adopt critical judgments made by other people about their children's character. Quotes that discouraged parents have shared with us include: "This kid is just jerking your chain." "She's a spoiled brat." "He's so lazy." "This kid is just evil." These statements can feed parents' anxiety and unhelpful responses unless they learn to "speak the truth in love" to themselves about their child.

"My child is my report card"

Parents often have unhelpful thoughts about a child if they have a subtle belief that their child's behavior is their report card. There is a tendency to think, "If my child behaves well, I am a good parent. If my child misbehaves, I am a bad parent."

Stated so bluntly, it's obviously not true, but it is still a powerful and subtle belief for nearly all parents. Getting their value from their child's behavior puts tremendous pressure on parents to control the child and pressure on the child to get it right. This usually has very negative results for the child and for the parent as they both ride an emotional roller coaster together, overreacting to the normal ups and downs of children's behavior.

Our son Noah was a lively, bright little guy, very inquisitive and often a bit impulsive. The day he got caught lighting matches in the church provided a good test of my (Jim's) ability to not allow my child's behavior to be a statement of my value or success as a parent. Apparently he and some friends had gathered under a stairway between services and Noah was lighting matches, spreading that distinct sulfuric odor throughout the area. I was quite embarrassed when I heard about it from, of all people, the pastor's wife. To make matters worse, one of the younger boys who had followed our little Pied Piper into this activity was her son.

Lynne and I are our church's endorsed parent educators. My credibility was at stake! "How could he do this, and in front of so many people?" was my thought. My first impulse was to find him and punish him so she would know that I had things under control, to save face. I learned long ago, however, that my first impulse is rarely a helpful response, so I took time to stop, calm myself and get perspective.

I was able to think more clearly after I settled down a bit. I could acknowledge that his behavior was not about me; it was mostly childish lack of judgment. I even said out loud, "Even parent-educators' kids misbehave." I could then focus on how to help him learn from this, not on how to reduce my embarrassment. I found him, and as we walked to a quiet place it was clear that he felt bad about it and was ready to discuss a plan to resolve the issue.

This experience brought me back to the memory of the church elder who had called me for advice years before, furious at the humiliation he felt over his rebellious son's outrageous behavior. It seemed clear that their conflict had escalated because of the extreme ways the man tried to control his son in order to save face in his congregation. If a child senses that the parents' responses are driven by a desire to protect their own reputation, not by what is good for the child, it can drive a wedge between them. Many parents we've spoken to have latched onto our phrase, "My child is not my report card," as a way to avoid getting their value from their child's behavior.

"I deserve peace, quiet, and an obedient kid!"

Particularly if a parent is going through a stressful time, an underlying belief that often triggers parental overreactions is some variation on (as silly as it sounds): "I have a right to peace and quiet, a compliant child, a supportive co-parent," etc. We overheard a young mom, Karra, angrily scolding her fussy toddler, "Just because you woke up at 5:30, does not give you the right to have a tantrum." We knew this mom was sometimes intensely frustrated by her son's lack of cooperation with her subtle but powerful belief that she deserved a full night's sleep, a well-behaved child, and a peaceful, low-stress life. When Lynne asked her, "What do you think Ethan would say to *you*?" She chuckled and admitted she was having a tantrum too.

Jack had a common variation on this "I deserve better" belief. I (Jim) asked him what his goal was when he came through the door after work. "I have a goal to come home to a clean house after a long day at the office. I think that's pretty reasonable." His frequent disappointment with the almost daily messes that greeted him resulted in harsh discipline of his son and criticism of his wife, Lyla, who was exhausted from parenting this difficult child. "You can't control how clean the house is," I said. "You can control how you enter the house. What kind of parent do you want to be when you come through the door?" His stern face softened, and he said, "I guess I want to be the kind that would love my kid and support my wife." When Jack changed his goal from something he couldn't control to something he could, he fairly quickly became less resentful and more graceful at home.

"Why can't my kid just do what she's supposed to do?"

One of the hardest parent-child combinations is a parent who is either a perfectionist ("get it right" personality) or a goal-oriented achiever ("get it done...now" personality), trying to raise an emotional or intense child who struggles in life. It is difficult for these parents to understand how their child can't just change her behavior and do what she knows is right.

Britt was a take-charge kind of person, and she was furious that she couldn't get control of her daughter Katie's disobedient and disrespectful behavior. She even had a few choice labels for her daughter during one of our early phone-coaching sessions, and then she continued her rant. "Why can't she just do what I ask her to do? Seriously, it's simple stuff like brush her teeth. Or leave her sister alone in the morning. Or, (her voice rising) BE QUIET WHILE I'M ON THE PHONE!"

I could hear Britt's muffled voice over the phone as she continued yelling, "For heaven's sake, Katie, STOP IT. I told you I was going to be on the phone. Can't you just be QUIET?"

I asked her if it was tough to be patient when her daughter was acting up. She said, "Absolutely. I've had it. My fuse is so short these days with her."

I summarized for her, "So she's frequently misbehaving, and you're frequently angry. It sounds like you're both stuck."

I decided to take a risk with this new client and gently asked, "As your coach, trying to help you with this problem, how might it impact your ability to change your behavior if I yelled at you, 'STOP IT. Can't you just be PATIENT?'"

"Oh, I get it," Britt responded gently. We began to dive into understanding the stress and discouragement that drove much of her daughter's misbehavior. Their relationship (and her daughter's behavior) was gradually transformed as Britt's compassion for her daughter grew and empowered her to have a gentler, more understanding response to the misbehavior.

"I don't deserve to be treated this way"

We hear many stories about children who constantly complain about or lash out at their parents in anger. "I hate you." "I wish I had different parents." Parents hearing these kinds of statements consistently report about how hurt they feel and how much they are tempted to retaliate. "What did we do to deserve this?" is their crying question. What these kids most need, however, is for their parents, instead of lashing back or crying in despair, to learn to not take their child's behavior personally—to let it slide like water off a duck's back.

To do this requires an understanding that the behavior is far less about the parent and far more about the child's stress. It could be an indicator of their discouragement, stress, anxiety, or simply the erratic behavior of a developing brain. Once parents learn to see it this way they can respond with compassion rather than with anger. This is not to say they don't address the misbehavior, but rather that it is addressed with grace and understanding rather than with anger and resentment.

Dan was livid over his adopted daughter's behavior. "It's terrible. She treats us like dogs." He and his wife, Carla, were truly suffering verbal and even physical abuse from Tina. This is an extreme case, but it beautifully makes the point about what is needed when a child's words and actions are hurtful.

Tina would mock them, tell them they were terrible parents, taunt them about anything that could get a rise out of them, and intermittently explode in vicious physical attacks. Carla and Dan were emotionally drained and feeling deeply hurt. They realized that their strong reactions fueled the repeating cycle, so they decided to focus on discovering what Tina really needed from them. They learned to see her hurtful behavior as a sign of her deep shame and pain, not her rejection of them.

During one particularly volatile episode, Dan endured Tina's rage for 30 minutes, all the while staying with her to protect her, to protect Carla, and to demonstrate a real-life model of Jesus' love that never leaves or forsakes. Where once Dan would have angrily confronted Tina, fueling yet another escalation, God now gave him compassion for her. This compassion compelled him to begin to pray for her softly. As he prayed, she softened. Her tense posture relaxed and she suddenly began to sob in remorse. Love had broken through. Over time Tina's abuse grew less and less frequent as she became more confident in their love for her.

When Anger Is More than Anger

Many parents report that they feel angry at their children. It is the emotion most often displayed during discipline. For most people anger is a more comfortable emotion because it feels more powerful and less vulnerable than emotions such as anxiety, confusion, sadness, shame, or hurt. We have seen that when parents are brave enough to look beneath the surface, they often discover that anger is a shield for other more vulnerable emotions. Getting to the root of these feelings is an important part of the work of letting your mind be renewed.

If anger is a common emotion, a helpful question to ask is, "What would I feel if I couldn't feel angry?" It will likely require some reflection or journaling to answer, but the answer can be quite revealing, and will help you think more deeply about how to manage those emotions.

Learning to Be Okay When My Kids Are Not

As important and wonderful as Bible studies and worship services are, home is the test of what's real in our lives. If we look to our kids to love us unconditionally or to act in ways that make us look good or feel good, their misbehavior will really push our buttons. Our over-reactions likely reveal that in some way we feel anxious, inadequate, or rejected, which actually means that we're dependent on our children to feel peaceful, adequate, and loved. It communicates to our children that "I'm not here for your needs; you're here for my needs," and that's a setup for disappointment. It puts unnatural burdens on children when they are responsible for their parents' sense of well-being.

When we believe God's love is enough, we can be okay even when our children are unkind or angry at us. When they watch us hang onto our sense of being loved and are okay in tough situations, they begin to learn that they can be okay even when life is tough or others are angry with them.

The Secret to Preparing My Heart

In the last analysis, preparing my heart is not just what I do to discipline effectively; it is what I do to know and walk in God's grace and truth. Truthfully, if parents can do this in their own homes, in the everyday challenges of real life with growing children, they can probably do it anywhere.

In John 8:32, Jesus said, "The truth will set you free." When I plant my feet firmly on God's truths about me and my child, I can be okay when my kids are not. I can stand strong and calm despite the craziest misbehavior. I can know the peace of God that surpasses understanding and I can learn the secret of being content in every circumstance (see Philippians 4). That's true freedom, because my children are not controlling my emotions. When I'm in control of my thoughts and emotions, I can choose how I want to respond instead of having knee-jerk reactions that really mean my kid is in charge. At the deepest level, this is what is needed if my heart is to be well-prepared for the challenges of disciplining my children.

Only because of God's love and his forgiveness through Christ am I full, complete, and deeply loved and *not* dependent on my kids to feel okay. The more I can remind myself of those truths, even in tense situations, the more my parenting changes from the ground up. Then I am "transformed by the renewing of [my] mind" (see Romans 12:2).

Here are some "grace and truth" beliefs that have helped hundreds of parents, including us, prepare their hearts:

- "My child is not my report card. The love of Jesus is where I get my value."
- "It is not my responsibility to make everyone happy. They are responsible for that."
- "This behavior is just a moment in time; it doesn't define my child or his future."
- "Jesus, you are always with us and full of mercy in our struggles."
- "My child and I are gifts to each other, given by God for His perfect purposes."
- "There's a significant opportunity in any challenge."

You can also consider these verses as you trust God to guide you in this process of preparing your heart (which by now you've figured out is really about spiritual growth):

- **Psalm 51:6,** "Surely You desire truth in the inner parts; You teach me wisdom in the inmost place."
- **Proverbs 24:3,** "By wisdom a house is built, and through understanding it is established."

In her book, *"She's Gonna Blow,"* Julie Barnhill tells us that God does not give us our kids so that we can "fix" them or whip them into shape. God gave us our children to make us more like Jesus. So, in a profound sense, my "disciplers" are actually running around the house, every day, eager to assist the Lord in my transformation process. This is good news. I don't have to purchase a large manual entitled, "The 12 Steps to Spiritual Growth." I'm off to a great start if I just identify the hurtful beliefs that get triggered when my child acts up, and then, by faith, I replace those beliefs with God's truth. This is faith in action, in my own home, for my whole family to watch and learn from. And, as important and wonderful and valuable as family devotion times can be, this kind of dependence on God brings faith to real life in a rich way.

SECTION TWO: "MY CHILD, YOU ARE LOVED... NO MATTER WHAT"

Chapter 7

Keeping the Message of Love Alive Even in Our Discipline

What might happen if every time Christian parents disciplined their children they would do so with consideration for these powerful verses from the Bible:

- "...that you, being rooted and established in love, may have power, together with all the saints, to grasp how wide and long and high and deep is the love of Christ" (Eph. 3:18).
- "How great is the love the Father has lavished on us, that we should be called children of God!" (1 John 3:1).
- "The goal of our instruction is love..." (1 Tim.1:5 NASB).
- "But God demonstrates his own love for us in this: While we were still sinners, Christ died for us" (Rom. 5:8).
- "God is love. Whoever lives in love lives in God, and God in them" (1 John 4:16).

Since God's very essence is love, it only makes sense that we practice God's love as we discipline our children.

One mom angrily responded after a seminar, "I tried saying 'I love you' when my daughter misbehaved, and it didn't work." Hmmm. If we say "I love you" or demonstrate love in order to get kids to behave, it's nothing more than manipulation. It's conditional. We couldn't help but wonder if her daughter recognized this not as true love, but as a new technique to control her disrespect.

Of course many parents tell us that even their harshest of consequences is delivered out of love for their children, their desire to teach right from wrong, or their effort to protect their children from even harsher, real-life consequences in the future. While we agree that firm discipline can be warranted and effective, we always ask parents what we think is the most important question: Is the firm discipline really working? Over time, is it producing children who are more confident, more respectful, and more loving toward others? If so, then our discipline is connecting and our kids are growing in our love and in a sense of God's love and purposes for them. But if not—if our children generally seem discouraged, defiant, disrespectful, and self-centered, and if problem behaviors are increasing, not decreasing—then it is likely that our love is not "landing" on them when they are disciplined. It could be that more must be done to assure the kids know our love.

Having said this, even well-disciplined children sometimes go into behavioral tailspins. After all, they are free to choose how to respond to discipline and how to behave. They get discouraged in spite of our best efforts. They forget that they are loved. We can't control this. But we can control our own attitude and actions. Like Jesus and the apostles, we can choose to show love, even when it's hard.

The Power of Love

Mitch hated math. His dad, Andy, a mortgage banker, reported that Mitch had always struggled with math and that by sixth grade he just couldn't seem to keep up. This troubled Andy greatly and so he put a firm rule in place that Mitch couldn't play with friends until his homework was done. It's a reasonable rule. But as a result, Mitch was getting less and less time with friends and growing more and more discouraged.

Early in the school year Mitch started lying that his math homework was done so that he could go out and play. But he got away with it only until the first phone call from his teacher. Andy loved Mitch and he was a great dad, but when he found out that very little math had been turned in he hit the roof. "No son of mine is going to behave this way. You're grounded on weekdays until you're back on track. And from now on I'm looking at every assignment before you leave the house."

The consequences Andy chose were reasonable given the circumstances. But Mitch grew increasingly disheartened as the math got more difficult. Andy would come home from work each day at about five o'clock and ask to see Mitch's homework. His other subjects were fine, but he never had his math done. He would make excuses, he would whine, and he would complain that math was dumb. Most nights would end in exasperation, and sometimes Mitch sobbed as Andy sat with him, trying to help his son get it. Andy would all but do the problems so that Mitch could turn in the work. Mitch grew increasingly ashamed, knowing that his dad was deeply disappointed. It was grating on every aspect of their relationship.

I (Jim) suggested to Andy that he make sure Mitch felt loved in the middle of all this. "Are you kidding?" Andy asked, almost in disbelief. "He knows I love him. Are you telling me that he should feel more loved when he's failing in math? That'll just make him think it's okay. And it's not." I asked Andy if he had any other ideas about how to help Mitch feel more encouraged. After conceding that he'd tried everything else, Andy reluctantly agreed to somehow express his love to Mitch.

"Just make sure," I encouraged, "that when you let him know you love him, you do it in a sincere way, not expecting or demanding a change in his behavior, or he will just feel manipulated." Andy nodded and said he'd report the outcome at the next session.

The Bible tells us that in the middle of our greatest sin, God loves us (Romans 5:8). Yet as parents we've somehow bought into a myth that if we let our kids know we love them when they are misbehaving, it will somehow reinforce the misbehavior.

Our experience is quite the opposite. We have found repeatedly that when parents can make their love known, even in the worst of behavior challenges, it almost always softens the intensity of their children's oppositional attitudes.

> When parents can make their love known, even in the worst of behavior challenges, it almost always softens the intensity of their children's oppositional attitudes.

When I saw Andy the following week his eyes were bright. "You wouldn't believe it." Andy started. "The day we last talked I prayed that God would help me to be more in tune with my love for Mitch in this whole math thing. That day, after work, Mitch was in fine form. He threw every excuse in the book at me. I was getting frustrated, but then I caught myself. Instead of launching in to set him straight the way I usually do, I just paused and let Mitch go on a while. I felt a new sense of compassion for him. Then it dawned on me, I really do love this little guy. He's my beloved son. I could sense a calmness I'd not felt in the middle of this before. Mitch could sense it too. 'What's with you?' he asked.

"I relaxed and sat down on the stairs where he'd met me, so that our eyes were on the same level. I looked Mitch in the eye and in the simplest of fashion said, 'Mitch, doing well in math is important. But do you know what's far more important?' I was kind of solemn. Mitch shook his head, not knowing what to expect. 'What's far more important is that you know how much I love you, and whether you are good at math or not can't change that.'

"Mitch's eyes filled with tears and he jumped into my arms and began to sob. 'I'm sorry, Dad! I'm just not very good at it.'

"'It's okay son.' I hugged him for a while and then asked Mitch if he wanted my help to get it done. He said that he did, and, while it was still hard for him, the resistant attitude I usually got was gone. He asked questions and worked harder than at any recent time. As the week went on, I did less of the math and he did more. Last night he did the assignment on his own and, when he finished, was proud to show it to me. I was gentler when I noticed some errors, and he was patient when I worked with him to correct those problems. He's a different kid. And, I have to admit, I'm a different dad."

Whether or not Mitch had changed his attitude or improved his math efforts, Andy could sincerely say that he was more satisfied with his approach to Mitch, having prepared his heart to express sincere love. In Andy's case, the change in approach made all the difference for Mitch.

Biblical Love in Discipline

Galatians 5:19–20 provides a list of "misbehaviors" (sins) that would be any parent's worst nightmare, including immorality, witchcraft, rage, drunkenness, and (last but not least) orgies. Then, in 5:22–23, there is a strong contrast: "But the fruit of the Spirit is love, joy, peace, patience, kindness, goodness, faithfulness, gentleness and self-control." The verses make a contrast: "This is sin. This is walking in the Spirit."

Then the first verse of the next paragraph (6:1) puts the two together, saying, "…if someone is caught in a sin, you who are spiritual should restore him gently." This exhortation seems to tie these contrasting ideas together by saying, "The gentle restoration is guided by the Spirit. Only when love, joy, peace, patience, goodness, kindness, faithfulness, gentleness, and self-control are put into practice, as the fruit of abiding in The Spirit, can these terrible problems be corrected." This isn't to say that there will be no consequences, but that the consequences will be guided and administered by the fruit of the Spirit. So if that's how to correct adults caught in extreme sin, doesn't it make good sense for parents to correct their children with the same spirit-filled, gentle discipline as well? After all, this is the approach the Lord uses with us. In Romans 2:4 we're told that "…God's kindness leads you toward repentance…"

Kindness in correction is not a magic bullet that quickly stops all misbehavior. We frequently talk with parents whose hearts are broken because, in spite of their best efforts to demonstrate their love, their children choose the path of rebellion. This can happen. It happened in the Garden with Adam and Eve. But though Adam and Eve rebelled, God kept on loving them. It happens in a certain sense with all of us. The Bible is clear: we have turned to our own way. We have rebelled against God's love. Some come out of their rebellion in response to God's love through Christ, and some do not. But God never stops offering his love, his kindness that leads to repentance.

After that model, we parents must find ways to prevent our hearts from getting jaded or resentful when our kids rebel. We must allow the Holy Spirit to nurture in us hearts of love and forgiveness so that we can confront misbehavior in the same way. Only when we do this hard work will we be able to love our children with God's love in a way that might reach their hearts and draw them back to God's love.

Chapter 8

"Love Casts out Fear"... Anxiety.... Discouragement.... Embarrassment...Shame....

Meet the Need Driving the Misbehavior

In our work with children and youth who are challenging to their parents, we almost always find that fear and/or discouragement is at the root of a child's chronic misbehavior. I John 4:18 tells us that perfect love drives out fear—the fear that may motivate much of a child's difficult behavior.

Consider this story from a family we coached regarding the constant whining of their adopted son, Bryan. It is an example how the common approach to something may not be the best approach, and how understanding, and helping our kids understand the root of their challenges can have great reward.:

> A few weeks ago my husband, Dan, read that the feeling behind anger is often fear. We talked a lot about how addressing the underlying fear puts the anger into perspective and makes it easier to deal with. We also talked about how this applied to our kids. I remembered Lynne's comment that our son Bryan seemed like an anxious child; his whining could be a way of coping with his anxiety. This idea stuck with me because I was frustrated and ready for some fresh perspectives.
>
> From early on in his development, Bryan would frequently whine in a high-pitched voice throughout the day. We read

all the books about how to manage the whining and tried it all. "Talk to me in a normal voice." "Go to time-out until you can use a regular voice." "You will lose your favorite 'stuffy' when you choose to whine."

We would mostly say these phrases without raising our voices and calmly follow through on the consequences we'd set. But at the end of the day there would be a great big pile of confiscated stuffed animals, and he would still be whining. In my weaker moments, I would become exasperated, hold out my hand and firmly say, "Stop, Bryan. Stop that whining voice." I knew that the intense energy I gave to making him stop was actually rewarding his whining, but I didn't know what else to do. Nothing ever worked—until we started seeing this new perspective.

The next day after our discussion about fear, Bryan was using that high-pitched voice because he could not find a DVD he wanted. Dan tried the "Stop whining," command, but the whining got worse. So we tried a whole new approach. I asked Bryan if he was scared that we would never find the DVD, and he softened and answered, "Yes." I said I would come down and look with him. I got distracted on the way and when he got impatient Bryan came to me with a super calm voice, "Mom, can you come help me find the DVD, please?" I about fell over. I praised him and took the chance to rephrase Philippians 4:6, 7, "Don't worry about anything...." We went right to the TV room and found the DVD. Wow, what a difference.

Since that eye-opening night, we've continued to address his underlying anxiety instead of his tone of voice. I calmly say things such as, "Wow! I can see you're really upset about that. It's hard to be upset, isn't it?" He doesn't always stop right away and I don't force it, but within a few minutes he almost always calms down and accepts some simple teaching or problem-solving about the situation.

This seems so simple, but we had been off base for five years. Since the DVD episode I have become more empathetic and affirming (rather than controlling), and he is whining less. He now has whole days when he doesn't whine at all. Yea, God! We talk at the end of the day about how much better life goes when he uses his regular voice and tries to figure out what makes him anxious or afraid. We keep talking about how only God can bring his peace when we acknowledge and give him our fears. Now instead of just trying to stop the whining, which wasn't working anyway, we are building faith, insight, and problem-solving skills that will last him a lifetime.

In this family's situation, the misbehavior was not what needed addressing. It was Bryan's underlying anxiety. The primary change needed was not behavioral but a change in the way these parents viewed the issue and helped their son start understanding some biblical perspective. Once those changes were made, the behavior improved dramatically.

We have seen children passionately and tenaciously stick to a lie because they are terrified of what will happen or what it means about them if they tell the truth. Or they scream criticism and blame on a parent because they are ashamed of their own failure. Or they act as though they don't care or are unmotivated because they are deeply discouraged, with no hope of success. The list goes on. But before I can effectively answer the question, "What should I do?" I need to ask, "What's going on with my child? How can I meet an underlying need that is driving this behavior?" This not only brings love and peace into the interaction but it helps my child learn to understand and deal with difficult emotions that are driving his misbehavior.

So if a child is stuck in a persistent behavior challenge, prayerfully consider what you might address in yourself or in your child that is below the surface of that behavior.

Expressing love and kindness during misbehavior or failure is the only way to truly convince our children that they are loved unconditionally—no matter what they do. Parents realize that expressing love is important, but they usually miss the opportunities when it's most important. For many parents this is a new idea. It's easy to grow accustomed to expressing frustration or anger when kids misbehave and reserving expressions of love for when kids do well or need comfort.

> Expressing love and kindness during misbehavior or failure is the only way to truly convince our children that they are loved unconditionally.

Simply stated, if the onlytime parents express love to their kids is when they perform well, or are hurting, the message communicated is that love is conditional. When kids begin to think that they are loved conditionally, they will do whatever they can to feel loved. If they can perform well, they will. If they can't, they will whine, or complain, or escalate to whatever misbehavior they can in order to at least get some kind of big reaction from their parents. In their eyes, a big angry reaction is much better than no reaction. Over time, these kids often turn to rebellion because of how discouraged they feel.

Build Emotional Security

If parents express love when their children are doing nothing in particular, however, (i.e., during neither significantly positive or negative behavior), they communicate to their children that they are loved just for who they are, not for what they do. If we imagine a bank account of emotional security in children's hearts, this would make a nice deposit in that bank account of feeling loved and valuable.

If parents will express love when their children are struggling or misbehaving, that is the most effective way to convince them that they are so valuable that they are loved *in spite* of what they do. This makes a large deposit in their bank account of emotional security, to prepare them for times when critical or untrue messages from the world around them attempt to make withdrawals from their sense of being loved and valuable.

The Kids Aren't the Only Ones Who Change

Early in our ministry, Melanie came into a parenting class with the label "angry mom" etched by the scowl lines on her face. She had grown up in a home where harsh yelling or punishment was the reaction to all misbehavior, whether childish or intentional. She rarely, if ever, felt as though she pleased her parents or was enjoyed by them. Even though Melanie had come to faith as an adult, this pattern of interaction was largely repeating itself in her family. She lost no time in telling us about her daughter's difficult behaviors and listened skeptically to our statements about "Connection in Correction"— letting misbehaving children know they are loved, no matter what.

That following week, her daughter, Anna, had disobeyed by playing with a soccer ball in the living room, near the antique family heirloom lamp that was her mom's most prized possession. As the soccer ball ricocheted into the fragile antique, it exploded into lamp shrapnel all over the floor. Melanie's instinct was to do the same, explode all over her daughter. As she started into that familiar rage response she for the first time ever noticed how fearful her daughter seemed, cowering on the floor awaiting mom's wrath. She felt a twinge of compassion and remembered the phrase, "Connection in Correction" she had learned in the class. She knew this was an opportunity demonstrate God's unconditional love, if she could just let go of her own rage. She dropped to her knees, gathered up her terrified daughter into her arms and from her newly found heart of compassion said said, "That lamp was really special to me, but I love you so much more than that lamp!" Relief poured out in Anna's deep sobs as her mom held and rocked her. Problem-solving about what to do about the lamp could wait.

Seven years later we connected with Melanie again, but this time she was vibrant and joyful. "That was absolutely a turning point in my life," she said. "I realized I didn't have to be the parent my parents were." She filled us in on the rest of the story. After the soccer ball incident Melanie and her daughter volunteered to do a dramatic presentation of the event. It was so well received that they ended up "touring" moms' groups around their community, performing the skit and sharing a message about the importance of "connection in correction," or the importance of expressing love when kids misbehave.

Saturating in this truth about God's love and grace began to heal the wounds from Melanie's childhood. She gradually fully forgave her parents for all their rage and rejection, joyfully expressed unconditional love to them, and eventually led her terminally ill mom to faith in Jesus Christ. For Melanie, this wonderful cascade of God's love and power that broke the pattern of generations all started with a simple decision: Let go of the anger (I prepare my heart) and communicate love, no matter what, to my struggling child.

Certainly Melanie's story is more dramatic than most, but many parents have reported to us the wonderful interplay between expressing unconditional love to their children and growing in their own understanding of God's passionate love and mercy for them when they struggle.

Chapter 9

Love No Matter What, Made Practical

Here are some simple, practical ways you can begin to communicate "Love, no matter what" when your children misbehave. While these may be simple changes, the prerequisite for their effectiveness is that a parent has prepared his or her own heart. Then these changes just take seconds to employ but can powerfully turn the tide of negative-discipline encounters:

- Get down on their level instead of towering over them.
- Touch them gently if they can receive it.
- Empathize—"I can see you are upset. I get upset like that too, sometimes."
- Verbalize "I love you."
- Repeat what you hear your children say. "So you are really upset with me."
- Look at them peacefully for a moment and smile.

Get Down on Their Level

Lynne and I once sat at a beautiful cherry wood table for one of those high pressure, very convincing timeshare sales presentations. In spite of our well-thought-through conviction that we would not buy, we found it extremely difficult to resist. We were about finished and feeling good about our resolve when the manager, "Slick Sam," came in all dressed up and with a sales quota to fill. He stood across from us and we looked up at him. With every objection we reviewed, he got a bit closer to us and assured us that our objection was invalid. Soon he was standing directly across the table, looming over us as we sat in cushy, but rather low leather chairs. It was nearly impossible to say "no" to him. It took all our fortitude to keep thinking rationally and resist Sam's crafty tactics. In the end it truly felt as though we had won a battle we hadn't even known we were getting into.

We later learned that standing posture is frequently employed as a high-pressure sales tactic. It turns out that it puts the sales person in an intimidating posture that is much more likely to coerce a decision to buy.

As it relates to misbehaving children, parents often loom over them, large and intimidating. Even our teens, though they may be our size or larger, tend to think of us as bigger and more powerful than they. So one powerful way we can communicate to our children that we are for them and not against them is simply to shrink our posture with them. This shrinking is best accomplished by sitting or kneeling so that the kids can either be level, or even look down at us. It also helps to take our hands off our hips, or uncross our arms, and consciously place our hands in an open position.

Gentle Touch—with Permission

Safe, affectionate touch is a powerful communicator of love. Saying, "We're both kind of upset now" and asking, "Would you like a hug?" can be calming and reassuring, giving parent and child a chance to reconnect and think more clearly. Lightly placing a hand on the shoulder of the child we are confronting can communicate our presence in the struggle with our children. It helps us to join them as coaches or mentors rather than as adversaries. This is usually quite effective if parents have no agenda, but not always. If either Lynne or I put a hand on Daniel's shoulder during an argument, and there was any hint of control, he reacted angrily.

Claire had three young children and was struggling with Tyler, her oldest. He was an intense and sensitive five-year-old who could have a meltdown over minor issues or changes in schedule. At Lynne's recommendation, Claire began to strongly increase the affectionate touch she provided during the day. A few weeks later Claire stated that she frequently avoided meltdowns with her sensitive son by affectionately rubbing his shoulders as he started to get upset. "I can't believe what a difference this has made." He responded well to this because she made a practice of doing this frequently when he wasn't upset, so the touch had positive connotations to him.

Empathy

When she was in 5th grade, Bethany and I (Lynne) were locked in a power struggle about a jungle-in-a-shoebox assignment. She was determined that we go to a certain craft store where her high-achieving classmate had bought some elaborate supplies. I knew we had what she needed at home, but she still demanded to go to the store. I did not want to feed into what I judged to be insecurity and competition with this classmate by unnecessarily going to the same store. But it didn't feel quite right to simply demand, "No! Now just deal with it." So we were stuck and the conflict continued to escalate.

At one point I stopped to get some perspective on what each of us was feeling. I prepared my heart and then said, "Are you kinda anxious about this project because you really want to do a good job? I know how it feels to want to measure up to classmates." I truly empathized, and she could sense that I wasn't just saying this to get my way. Immediately her intensity relaxed. I continued, "I'm glad you work hard on your assignments. How about if we get started with what we have and if you don't feel good about the result, we'll go to the store tomorrow." With a little understanding and affirmation

I went from being her opponent to her teammate. She eagerly got started on her project with the supplies we had and felt great about the end result.

This principle of empathy, to identify with and validate feelings, is a helpful way to connect with struggling children, from toddlers to teens. Take your best guess at what they might be feeling and make an observation or simply ask them. When the toddler who lives in our basement with his single mom starts to pitch a fit and pound his high chair tray before a meal, we emphatically say in simple kid language, "You're hungry. You want food. You want food. Mommy's getting it." It's amazing how much that helps him to calm down. Another mom reported that immediately following one of our workshops, with these thoughts fresh in her mind, she tried this with her tantrumming child. "I simply said, 'You're really mad right now. You wanted to stay and play.' I was shocked by how well it worked, and how this approach has worked ever since."

> When I can identify with and communicate my understanding of my children's feelings, it helps them to know that I'm on their side.

Empathizing with misbehaving children is quite counter-intuitive. To empathize is to let your child know that you feel what she feels, that you identify with her feelings and understand those feelings. When I can identify with and communicate my understanding of my children's feelings, it helps them to know that I'm on their side. It also helps them to get in touch with their own feelings, which switches the strong activity in their brain from the reactive, self-protection parts of the right brain to the left side which specializes in language and logic. Studies show that the more children are able to express their feelings, the less aggressive they are.

Expressing feelings verbally gives children a more helpful outlet for their feelings and is the first step toward rationally problem solving. So empathizing not only helps in the short run, it helps children learn to better sort out and deal with their heavy feelings in the long run.

Really Listening to My Child

When my child feels that he is being heard, he feels respected. When he feels respected, he is far less inclined to continue down defiant paths. Rephrasing what I hear my child say requires that I am listening, more interested in his perspective than my own at that point. And doing this helps me to makes sure that I've understood him. This helps my child to feel respected and switch his response from explosive to evaluative as he figures out if I really understand what he is trying to say.

Sometimes our kids just need us to be quiet for a little while. One day, Daniel loudly expressed some intense frustration over a situation for which I (Lynne) was partly responsible. I parked on the top step of our basement stairs while he vented emphatically from the landing below. He was bordering on being disrespectful and, normally, I would have likely stopped him to firmly let him know my perspective. But this time I didn't have a clue about what to say or how to solve the problem. I almost felt like God had his big, gentle hand across my mouth, protecting Daniel from a potential condescending lecture. So I sat and said absolutely nothing as I listened and smiled gently to express my understanding. The more I listened the more rational he became. When he finished, he stared back at me for a few seconds. I still had nothing to say, but he apparently felt quite satisfied and walked off and constructively solved his problem.

Verbalize "I love you"

This may seem obvious, but give it a try. For us to tell our kids we love them takes a sincere heart of love, not manipulation. Its helpfulness grows from a foundation of expressing this message frequently at other times when kids aren't misbehaving.

Getting in touch with your heart of love for your children while they are misbehaving requires a powerful act of faith. Like the parents in the stories earlier in this chapter, we believe that if you can make a habit of this, you will begin to see different outcomes with your children.

Chapter 10

When Love Begins to Rule:
The Eternal Impact

Perhaps the most significant benefit of communicating "Love, No Matter What" when our children misbehave is that it paves the way for children to truly understand God's love for them. Romans 8:38–39 reads, "For I am *convinced* that neither death nor life, neither angels nor demons, neither the present nor the future, nor any powers, neither height nor depth, nor anything else in all creation, will be able to separate us from the love of God that is in Christ Jesus our Lord." This is a wonderful but lofty verse for children to understand.

Imagine if they experienced and truly believed, "For I am convinced that neither my failure nor lying, neither tantrums nor defiance, neither whining nor complaining, nor any disrespect, neither forgetfulness nor messes, nor any other misbehavior will be able to separate me from my mom's and dad's love and the love of God that is in Christ Jesus my Lord."

> Parents who want their children to desire to walk in God's love and truth would do well to consider an important question: How do I want my child to view God when she messes up?

Parents who want their children to desire to walk in God's love and truth would do well to consider an important question: How do I want my child to view God when she messes up?

One of our coaching clients, a young dad named Ted, shared his story about a great opportunity for abounding grace and a lifelong lesson about the character of God.

> I was working hard to encourage my seven-year-old daughter, Liddy, in her piano practice. But she was having a rough day, and it spiraled into a huge meltdown. As she was shouting and screaming, I subtly began to video tape her outburst on my cell phone. I wanted to use it to build insight in a grace-filled way, so I waited until we connected that night at bedtime. I showed Liddy the video tape and asked her if she liked feeling that way. Seeing herself on the video clip, Liddy was discouraged and ashamed. "Daddy, I don't like seeing that."
>
> This is where parents typically might say something like, "Liddy, if you don't like how you acted, you can choose to respond differently next time."
>
> The Lord helped me to see Liddy's struggles with eyes of compassion. I saw a great opportunity to shape her heart with a valuable spiritual truth. I explained that because of what Christ has done for us, when we ask forgiveness of others and God, He forgets our sins and doesn't look back. "It's like God erases the tape," I explained. Then I asked if she wanted to say anything. She looked up and said, "I want your forgiveness and God's forgiveness. And I want to erase the tape." I let her watch me hit the delete button, and Liddy smiled in relief as the vivid reminder of her failure disappeared. As we said bedtime prayers she thanked God for his forgiveness.

Liddy is an intense little girl, and although she is growing more able to control that intensity, she still struggles. As her parents persist at responding with grace when times are tough, Liddy is learning in real time about a God who loves her even at her worst and is there to forgive and love her in all circumstances. These are the kinds of moments through which parents can have a unique and intimate influence in their children's hearts that no Sunday school teacher or youth worker could ever have.

When love is consistently expressed this way in families, the love begins to define household life. There will still be squabbles and challenges. Kids will still argue and parents will still get harsh. But with the priority of communicating love, parents will also know when they've missed the mark. They will model humility in asking forgiveness for unneeded or disrespectful harshness. True reconciliation will happen. Then, as parents become more thoughtful about how to talk out loud about God's love for us in the midst of our worst behavior, children are discipled in a most powerful way.

SECTION THREE: "YOU ARE CAPABLE... OF WISE BEHAVIOR"

Chapter 11

A Purpose-filled Process

The sibling conflict in our home was off the charts when our children were little, and frequently I felt like it pushed me (Lynne) to the edge of sanity. Daniel, the oldest, had been picked on by older neighbor boys. He used the social skills he had learned from his chums to intimidate and harass his brother and sister. He also was extremely strong-willed and was determined to be in charge of his younger siblings, if not the whole family. Bethany, three years younger than her brother, was very sensitive and had perfected the victim role in their relationship. We all played our parts in a well-choreographed dance: he bossed, taunted, or hit; she whined, wailed, or screamed; and I entered as Crazy Mama ready to punish the one with the criminal record. Though I knew my kids were precious miracles, created for God's glory, I totally lost sight of this when they fought. Here's an example:

From the basement came familiar sounds. "Bethany, stop it. You can't touch my Legos. You dummy, you broke it." Whack. At the sound of her piercing scream and ensuing sobs, I swooped down the steps like a missile programmed for one target—Daniel the tyrant. Seeing that Bethany was not hurt, I ignored her and grabbed him by the shoulders and yelled in his face, "That is not okay. Go to the time-out bench for ten minutes. Why are you so mean to her all the time?" He yelled back, "It's her fault. She broke my Explorian Starship. You're the mean one. You always just protect her. It's not fair." As he served his time on the bench, his anger at both of us boiled for the full ten-minute sentence. Soon, after the punishment, they were at it again for a different reason. I knew I needed to change my reactions to this kind of thing, because it was quickly spiralling out of control.

My first step in changing these unhelpful dynamics was to look below the surface and "prepare-my-heart." I recognized that part of my energy about this had nothing to do with Daniel but with my own past. As a youngster I was teased and occasionally harassed by older brothers. It was not excessive, but I hated how it felt and it never was really resolved well. I realized I was targeting Daniel with my judgments about older brothers who picked on poor, innocent, little sisters.

I confessed to Daniel that he was getting some leftover resentment I had toward my brothers, and asked his forgiveness. I started working at consciously setting down that baggage before I engaged with my children. This helped me enter with a little less anger and a little more "love, no matter what," and empathy and understanding for how hard it was for them to get along.

The most significant change happened when I learned to enter the fray with the question, "What's the opportunity here?" foremost in my thoughts. Jim and I began to discipline with the long-term view in mind instead of just trying to stop the short-term behavior. We had a desire for our children to develop the affection, empathy, and conflict-resolution skills that would serve them well in their families, workplace, and ministry. With this question in mind I now had a long-term purpose in mind for my discipline.

We didn't stop using consequences, but we tried first to find and strengthen whatever was right instead of immediately punishing what we thought was wrong. For example, were they using "gentle hands" in spite of their harsh words? Were they standing up strongly for what was important to them? I wanted to see and affirm these things while also addressing the sin.

We also used questions and choices to guide them through resolving their own conflicts. We would ask, "Do you want to solve this respectfully now or do you think you need to calm down first? How much help do you need to do that?"

This approach gave them the message that "You are capable," instead of, "You are a problem." Their conflict no longer represented an interruption in our peace and quiet, but it represented a great opportunity to disciple our kids in God's purposes for their lives.

It was a long process of ups and downs for all of us and on many days we wondered if we were getting anywhere, but it eventually paid off. Our children grew to be great friends and even started a small business together. As a college student negotiating life on her own, Bethany recently said, "I get along with everybody and can resolve conflict with anyone. I've got Daniel to thank for that!"

No Quick Fixes or Magic Bullets

At parenting workshops we often ask the question, "What's a typical goal when you discipline your child?" Here are the most common answers that parents give:

- To make the bad behavior stop.
- To get our kids under control.

A parent's dream would be to find one "magic bullet" technique that stops misbehavior immediately and works every time and in every situation. Stopping misbehavior is not necessarily a bad goal, but it focuses only on what's wrong and does little, if anything, to open children's hearts to God's grace and truth.

Jesus had a powerful ability to look beneath the people's presenting problems to see and imagine how those people could serve the Kingdom. He didn't treat "misbehavior" with an eye to just correct misbehavior, but with an eye for the changed hearts of those he confronted. His approach to confronting was almost always unique (no formula!). His consistency in confronting sin was not in his methods but in his faithfulness to respond from a place of peace and oneness with the Father, with the goal of changed hearts.

Consider how Jesus responded to adultery. In Luke 7:37 and following, he receives a prostitute's anointing, her tears, and her love.

> Jesus' consistency in confronting sin was not in his methods but in his faithfulness to respond from a place of oneness with the Father.

He then forgives her sins, with never a word of rebuke. She leaves a changed (saved!) woman, her heart forever changed. In John 4:7 and following Jesus meets the woman at the well and offers her "living water!" He offers no chastising, only a truthful and compassionate rendering of her sins. She is amazed and goes to her town, sharing her testimony of faith and inviting her neighbors to come hear him. Again, a changed heart! In John 8:3 and following Jesus protects the adulterer from the accusations of the angry crowd who want to stone her. After powerfully turning the crowd away with the invitation, "If any of you is without sin, let him be the first to throw a stone," Jesus invites the woman to leave her life of sin. Again—no punishment. Just wisdom and grace. No formulas. No magic bullets. Just changed hearts. This was *always* Jesus' goal.

Although the lack of a "magic bullet" to deal with misbehavior might sound like bad news, it's actually good news. It forces us, like Jesus, to be watchful, prayerful, dependent on God, and discerning about what's really going on with our children. From this thoughtful, faith-filled approach flows powerful influence in their lives.

Because of this perspective, the ideas suggested in this book will become valuable tools in a parent's tool box. It is up to the parent to discern which tool(s) will most benefit their unique child given the particular situation. For example, one child may first need empathy to know her parent understands. Another may benefit from some affirmation before addressing the misbehavior. Still another may simply need firm chastisement and some reasonable choices. No formulas. Always looking for heart change.

Thinking Long-term for Kingdom Purposes

Ephesians 2:10 says, "For we are God's workmanship, created in Christ Jesus to do good works, which God prepared in advance for us to do." The goal of hearts changed and invited into God's "good works" is enhanced when parents focus on long-term, "big picture" thinking instead of disciplining with a focus on simply punishing misbehavior to make it stop quickly. This kind of thoughtful discipline helps children understand God's purposes for them and builds the values and skills necessary to walk fully in these purposes. Parents can find and build these strengths in a child, even in misbehavior. Consider the differences in the following discipline examples:

Scene 1 - Typical discipline:

"Jordan, get your shoes on. It's time to leave," his mother, Lynette, instructs. She's feeling rushed about getting him out the door.

But Jordan, intent on his Lego creation, becomes defiant and lashes out. "No, Mommy! I'm making a truck. I don't wanna go."

Lynette feels challenged and firmly says, "Jordan, you obey me right now and get your shoes on or you're going to lose those toys."

Jordan knows Lynette means business, so he reluctantly decides to put on his shoes. He's learned that Mommy is still more powerful than he is and that he'd better do what she says. This is not a bad lesson to learn. But it is merely discipline and not discipleship.

Here's how his mom might take advantage of the discipleship opportunity:

Scene 2 - Discipleship Opportunity

Here the mother is looking for capability and calling it out:

"Jordan, get your shoes on it's time to leave..."

"No, Mommy, I'm making a truck. I don't wanna go."

Lynette recognizes an opportunity for teaching some important lessons. She looks at Jordan and with the hint of a smile says, "It's hard to obey sometimes, isn't it, Jordan? God sure made you creative and persistent." She pauses and prays silently, "Lord, how will you use these gifts in him?"

Lynette makes this offer, "Jordan, before you get your shoes on, show me this cool thing you're working on." Because she feels safe to him, Jordan is pretty eager to please his mom and he proudly displays the truck. "Wow, that's awesome! I love the huge wheels and the extra light on top. You can set it here on the table to remind you to finish it later. Do you want to put on your sandals or your tennis shoes?" Jordan may still remain defiant and end up losing the toys as a consequence, but Lynette's heart is now that of a "discipler." She is with him not against him. She believes he is capable of obeying and of creating, and she works with him to encourage obedience.

We can see the difference between scene one and scene two. In scene one Lynette's goal was quick discipline, and she engaged with a posture of control. In scene two she was still conscious of the immediate situation, but she was looking for opportunities to mentor her child by bringing out the best in him. As a result she noticed two things: The first was simply the abilities Jordan demonstrated, even in his misbehavior, and how God might use those capabilities in the future ("God sure made you creative and persistent!"). The second was how she could set him up to make a wise choice ("Before you get your shoes on, show me this cool thing you're working on," and... "Do you want to put on your sandals or your tennis shoes?"). She made it easy for him to choose to put on his shoes as requested, not forcing him but encouraging him to make a wise response. While she didn't let him off the hook for his misbehavior, she demonstrated that she was with him and not against him.

In Hebrews 12:10, the Bible states God's goals when he disciplines: "God disciplines us for our good, that we may share in his holiness." As I seek to follow the example of my Father, the first part of the verse challenges me to discipline my children truly for their good, not for my relief or desire to regain control. The second part of the verse invites me to consider how the discipline is leading my child toward holiness, or God's set apart or supremely distinct purposes for his or her life.

The key to responding to misbehavior this way is to view my children as both sinners *and* as miracles created in God's image and for God's purposes. Only then can I begin to see them first and foremost as capable of great things, despite their current misbehavior.

Chapter 12

Discovering Diamonds in the Rough

We are all created in God's image. We can't escape this fact. Of course there is a pressing problem—sin. We're all born into it and it complicates and covers God's image in us, putting a selfish spin on everything we do. Even when we have become "new creations in Christ" (see 2 Corinthians 5:17) we carry around the baggage of sin. So, as Paul says in Romans 7:21, "When I want to do good, evil is right there with me."

It is good to call sin out and to help my children understand its power in their lives. But when my children misbehave, if all I do is focus on and punish the sin without calling out the goodness and image of God in them, children begin to identify themselves with the sin, the misbehavior, or the problem they seem to be. When this happens, the children either openly rebel or develop shame and resentment that makes them want to hide their sin from parents and ultimately from God. This makes true repentance difficult, if not impossible. To help my children truly repent and turn away from their sin, they need a vision for what to turn toward, acting like the child of God they were created to be.

Looking for the Gift beneath the Sin

One of the most powerful ways to do this is to look for the gift gone awry—the God-given talent that is coming out twisted by sin and selfishness. Because of the intense developmental changes in growing brains, young children and teens are busy trying to figure themselves out. They tend to be quite self-focused, so their gifts and strengths are usually used to benefit themselves. Misbehavior can actually give parents some of the best insight into their child's potential strengths.

Simply stated, it takes skill to misbehave. A child's skill in and of itself is a gift from God. The way the skill is used determines whether or not a child sins. So I have a great opportunity when my child misbehaves to see beneath the sin and identify a skill, recognizing that if the skill is used the way God intended, this brings God glory. Even in misbehavior, I can call out the image of God in my child by seeing and calling out the skills God gave.

Kari, the single mom who lives with us, shared her own growth in this perspective. "Today Eli was whining for something over and over again. I realized he was being really persistent. I actually enjoyed wondering how God might use that strength some day. It helped me to be calm when I responded to him." This insight will enable her to affirm Eli's persistence as he grows and help him to use it more in alignment with God's purposes.

> It takes skill to misbehave. A child's skill in and of itself is a gift from God. The way the skill is used determines whether or not a child sins.

Seeing and affirming a child's gift in the middle of a stressful situation is no easy task. Paul wrote Philippians 4:8 when he was in prison, facing frequent beatings and not knowing if this would be his last day. In the midst of this awful reality he penned these powerful words, "...whatever is true, whatever is noble, whatever is right, whatever is pure, whatever is lovely, whatever is admirable—if anything is excellent or praiseworthy—think about such things." Or, as the NASB version states, "let your mind dwell on these things."

We decided early in our parenting to do our best to let our minds dwell on whatever we saw in our children that was right or pure, or praiseworthy. This fits with the common adage about encouraging kids—"Catch them being good." We took it a step further, though, and decided that even when our kids were misbehaving, because they were created in God's image and for God's purposes, if we looked hard enough, we could find something "excellent" or "praiseworthy." This helped us to be calmer when we disciplined and to keep a more balanced, hopeful perspective of our child. Over time we found that this approach revolutionized the outcomes of our discipline.

Through most of his childhood, Daniel argued intensely to make sure he got whatever he perceived as fair treatment. "That's not fair." "I didn't get as much ice cream." "You are always on Bethany's side." "I'm older; I should get a later bedtime." "Bethany and Noah don't have to do this much work." He could present his case with all the logic, detail, passion, and persistence of a great lawyer, exhausting any adult who happened to be his caregiver. Lynne's brother once observed, "It's like arguing with a really ticked-off little adult."

Over time, as we persisted in helping Daniel understand the feelings and perspectives of other people, he began to be concerned about fairness for others also and took on the role of "Impulsive Champion of the Underdog." He would rush into a conflict between his brother and sister, quickly decide which one was most at fault and administer "justice" by whacking that sibling.

As he matured in the Lord, that passion for justice, which we did our best to affirm even when it was coming out twisted, eventually developed into a deep sense of justice and compassion for hurting people. As a 21-year-old volunteer in Peru, Daniel raised thousands of dollars to help an impoverished clinic and has developed values and career aspirations to minister to oppressed populations.

It's a sequence we've seen in numerous kids whose parents are willing to look below the surface to notice and nurture the good in their misbehaving child. The gift appears first selfishly, then clumsily on behalf of others, then, over time, filled with grace and wisdom. Identifying these gifts not only connects with your child's heart but is a key way to turn discipline situations into discipleship opportunities.

Here's how a couple of common misbehaviors might be addressed in a typical fashion, and then how they might be addressed by parents with a vision for the fact that their child is created in God's image, fully capable of accomplishing God's purposes.

Common Misbehavior: Ryan is angry about not getting to use the car. He spews loudly, "I've been telling you all week that this is really important to me. I just wanna go out for a little while to see this movie and I hate your stupid rules about having homework done first. No other parents are so old-fashioned with their kids. Why don't you just get with it?"

Typical Parent's Response: "How many times have I told you not to talk to me that way? If you keep this up, you'll not only miss the movie tonight, but you'll be grounded from the car for the rest of the week."

Following this response a child usually feels attacked. If he thinks he has a chance of winning, he'll fight harder. If not, he'll give in and take his anger out either later or on someone or something else. In neither case does he feel respected or heard. What he learns is that his parent has all the power—for the moment. While he may learn that he has to behave better in order to get privileges, he is not likely to internalize the value of behaving properly because it's the right thing to do.

Affirming Response: "Ryan, you're really being honest about some strong feelings, which is a good thing. I really do want to hear what you have to say when you're calm enough to use a more respectful tone. Maybe we can work something out. Do you want to take a break for a bit or are you ready now?"

Following this response a child tends to feel heard and respected. His disrespectful attitude was addressed, and he is still accountable for it, but not in a way that caused him to feel attacked. He may not be happy, but he will likely choose to settle down and talk appropriately (unless this is a new way of being handled, in which case he may dig in his heels and try harder to get his way by carrying on). Even if he doesn't settle down, the fact that the parent's approach has been level-headed and respectful will make it easier for him to understand that his continued defiance is about him and not about an irrational, insensitive parent.

What Ryan learns is that he can negotiate if he's respectful and that his parents believe he can work it out. When he is calm his parents can help him to see that his honesty and strong will are abilities God gave him.

Common misbehavior: First-grader Hailey is about to leave the mess of markers and crayons all over the table to go play with other toys. The rule has been frequently stated that "We clean up one mess before making another or we lose the toys that we left."

Typical response: "Hailey! Where are you going? You'd better clean those markers up right now if you don't want to lose them."

Hailey may or may not clean up the markers. What she learns is that her parent is responsible for keeping the rules, not Hailey.

Affirming response: When Hailey gets down from the table, her dad, Jeff, lets her go. He waits to see if Hailey will clean up before playing with other toys. When Hailey starts with the other toys, Jeff goes to the markers and begins putting them in the "time-out bag." He invites, "Hailey, I'd like you to come over here while I pick up these markers for a time-out."

Hailey immediately complains, "No, Daddy. I want my markers."

"Hailey, you really love doing art don't you?" Jeff affirms. "I love that God made you to be able to bless others with your art. But it's important to be responsible with those art abilities. So you can help me clean up the markers right now and we can make it a one-day time-out instead of two. Do you want to help?"

Hailey learns that she is responsible for keeping the rules and that consequences will be put in place if she doesn't keep them. She also learns that Dad believes in and wants to support her talents.

Practical Examples

To help with specific applications of this idea, here is a list of common misbehaviors and some gifts/talents we have discovered that tend to drive them.

- Arguing/Backtalk = Honest with feelings and opinions, confident. (Research has shown that argumentative children are less likely to lie or be deceitful. In the long run they are more likely to adopt the values of their parents because they passionately exchange ideas instead of going underground with their perspectives.)
- Yelling = Expressive, desire to be understood

- Stubbornness = Determined, intensity of focus
- Bossy/strong will = Leadership/assertiveness
- Lying = Creative, good memory, likes to keep the peace
- Stealing = Planner, courageous, able to take risks
- Irritable = Sensitive
- Insecure = Aware of the feelings and perspectives of others
- Impulsive = Lives in the moment, quick responder
- Whining = Persistent
- Complainer = Aware of problems, potential for good problem-solving
- Defensive = Strong sense of right and wrong. (Kids that have the hardest time admitting guilt are usually those who feel the worst about having done something wrong)

We encourage parents to experiment with affirmation as they identify what might be the "gift gone awry." To get started, here are a few suggestions about how a parent might respond with affirmation when the misbehavior is whining or demanding behavior:

- "You are a very determined person. That's great."
- "You really know what you want."
- "I can see you really like..." (Whatever it is they're wanting).

When parents learn to respond this way, their children tend to calm down. Perhaps they feel surprised, or maybe they're used to feeling attacked and this feels more encouraging. Be sure, however, to communicate in a way that affirms the gift but not the behavior. After all, your child would really look at you quizzically if you said, "Nice job whacking your little brother."

Then, as the kids calm down, you can facilitate further success.

JIM & LYNNE JACKSON

For example:

- "Nice work calming down. When you're calm it makes it easier to talk."
- "It seems like you know some other ways to ask for what you want."

As these kinds of responses and statements become more normal, your kids will feel more respected and will gradually learn more respectful ways of navigating their way through conflict. You may even be the recipient of this kind of respect.

By the time Daniel was in his early twenties, he had learned to keep quite a cool head in conflict. One day he confronted me (Lynne) respectfully when I was somewhat "anal" about details of his photography business—clearly his business, not mine. Instead of reacting defensively, he took a deep breath, smiled, and gently said, "Mom, I appreciate your concern about my photography. How you're showing that concern right now is not very helpful." I realized I was nagging a young adult in charge of his own life and thanked him for the grace he dispensed. He replied with a grin, "I learned it from you, ya know."

In the heat of the moment we often missed seeing our children's gifts beneath the misbehavior, but when tempers cooled a bit, identifying those strengths was a really helpful way to regroup, regain perspective, and even have a "Do-over." For example, "I've been thinking about our conflict. I really appreciate your (honesty, strong convictions, sensitivity, etc.), and would like to try that conversation again." This dynamic helps create a momentum toward increasingly effective discipline that connects with a child's heart.

Position the Gift for Good Purposes

Another profound discovery we made in our years of working with high-risk teens was the powerful dynamic of identifying gifts gone awry and positioning the gift to be used for good purposes.

For example, if my child yells mean words, I can affirm his expressiveness, "Son, you are so expressive. I wonder if you could be expressive in a more helpful way." This doesn't let him off the hook for his mean words; it just paints a vision for how he could use his gift more constructively. Now he gets to choose. Many times, given this choice, a child will calm down and try another way instead of escalating the conflict.

This might sound crazy, but many of the teens who eventually made decisions to follow Christ at the outreach center where we worked looked to the way they were handled when they acted up as critical steps in their journey to discover God. Christa was one of them.

I (Jim) once left a building to round up kids for the meeting and stumbled on Christa, who was yelling abusively at Hannah. Her string of profanities and interjected verbs and nouns would have made a sailor proud. But I'm no sailor, and I was far from proud. I grew immediately flushed and my impulse was to yell loudly at her to "stop that abusive language right now!" I could feel the heat in my face and I knew that if I spoke it could be disrespectful. So I prayed quickly, "Lord, give me your grace." Had Christa been physically threatening, I'd have acted quickly, but she was not, and as I slowed my pace and approached her from behind, Hannah's eyes bulged as she saw me over Christa's shoulder. Christa immediately stopped, sensing Hannah's new discovery (me) and spun around.

Christa looked at me and sheepishly asked, "Am I kicked out?" She knew that the published consequence for her infraction was a one month "time-out" from programs and an apology to Hannah before returning.

I would have been fully justified in saying, "You know the rules. Yes, you'll have to take a break." But God's spirit seemed to be whispering to me a different way to handle this (and I have learned over the years to enjoy the treasure hunt of looking for God's purposes revealed through misbehavior). I said, "Christa, taking a break for a while is one way we could handle this, but I need to let you know that I've never seen such a powerful and creative use of those words before. You are one amazing communicator."

This took both Christa, Hannah, and even me a bit by surprise. It changed the whole tone of the interaction. What had been a highly charged and defensive interaction was now a curious and open conversation. Wanting to be sure Hannah felt supported, I offered, "Hannah, Christa will have to resolve things with you no matter what, but then I'm wondering if it's okay with you to offer her a little different consequence instead of just booting her?" Hannah was fine with it.

"So, Christa," I continued, "I want to offer you a choice of consequences. The first choice is to follow the normal rules for this kind of thing and give you a one-month time-out from programs. The second is that you can put that gift of yours, the way you communicate so well, to use here. So for the next month you could meet with me early each week and help prepare the announcements and the promotional fliers we make for our activities. I think that would be a much better way to use the gifts God gave you for communicating, don't you?" She nodded. "So which consequence do you choose?"

"The second one," she humbly offered. "And Hannah, sorry for cussin' you out like that. I've had a tough week."

"It's cool." Hannah replied. We went inside and the gals were quite chummy the rest of the night and for weeks to come.

The Power of this Approach

Over the next four weeks I followed my plan to involve Christa in the writing and speaking of announcements, something she continued for several months. She grew in those weeks to be much more protective of the environment of respect at the outreach center and emerged as a leader in the program. As she used her communication skills to serve the outreach, we noticed and affirmed how blessed we felt to have her help out that way. Her sense of purpose increased and she became more open to hearing about other ways God might use some of the gifts he'd given her. Her heart opened to all the things we taught—including the Gospel. Today she is following Jesus and raising her children to respect and serve others.

What I took away from this encounter with Christa is that there can be great power in finding ways to affirm the God-given traits that show up in misbehavior and then positioning those gifts to be used more in alignment with God's purposes.

Whenever we can find ways to affirm kids—not "You are great" but, "Your gift/talent really blessed me"—we remind them of the masterpiece God created them to be and the "good works they were created in advance to do." This can only serve to open their hearts to the greater purposes of God for their lives.

One of the most effective approaches to our son Daniel's bossiness of his siblings was not to jump into the situation and tell him how to treat his siblings. We certainly tried that with no success; i.e., "If you boss them, I'll boss you." We began to remind him that his strong personality included leadership potential for God's purposes. We also asked him a thought-provoking question: "What kind of approach do you want to practice to prepare you for these possibilities?" When he sensed that we were truly trying to help him rather than just control him, we could guide him with more questions that helped him learn to facilitate a group activity wisely. It has been very rewarding to watch him grow as an effective leader.

Speaking to your child in this way is not the hard part. Most parents can learn the scripts and repeat the words. The hard part is that in order to do that with sincerity, you have to believe it. You have to believe that your child is a gift, a miracle, created for important purposes—"For we are God's "workmanship," or "masterpiece," created in Christ Jesus to do good works, which God prepared in advance for us to do" (Eph. 2:10).

This can be quite difficult when our children misbehave. But if, when they misbehave, we can fairly consistently deal with them in grace and truth, with a vision for their lives, their hearts are most likely to open to God's grace and truth. So our work as parents is less about learning the right scripts and more about relentlessly nurturing a vision for God's purposes in our children. This is a key perspective in finding the discipleship opportunity in discipline situations.

Chapter 13

Facilitating Wise Choices

For children to grow up fulfilling God's purposes, despite the crazy culture around them that is only a mouse-click away, a parent's job also includes persistent, insightful training in making wise choices. A child needs to learn sooner, rather than later in life, to make wise choices when the pressure is on and emotions are intense. If parents are committed to this goal for their child, misbehavior is an unparalleled opportunity to build these great skills.

This can start at a young age with something as irritating as whining. Whining is a common problem, whether children are toddlers or teens demanding to get what they want. One thing is pretty predictable. When parents focus on controlling their child it usually backfires because it robs the child of any healthy sense of power. He may be intimidated into compliance but more likely will persist in the whining until he has pushed Mom or Dad over the edge—essentially controlling his parent. Offering choices to a child helps him to begin the process of controlling himself. It also helps him to learn that in tough situations there are always options.

Two-year-old Eli (our "housemate") whined and cried every morning at the bottom of the stairs. He wanted to be carried, but Kari kept trying to get him to go up the stairs on his own. She viewed it entirely as an obedience problem—he was disobeying her command. "Eli, come up the stairs. You can do it. I'm not going to carry you." The whining persisted and on most days escalated to screaming. In order to make it to work on time, Kari often stormed back down the stairs and hauled him up, complete with an angry scolding. This gave lots of attention to his behavior and perpetuated the problem. Warnings and time-outs did nothing to curb his stubbornness.

We talked with Kari about the value of teaching Eli to make wise choices and how to offer him two simple choices: "Eli, you can stay there and whine as long as you'd like [she was allowing extra time in their schedule], or you can come up the stairs and be with me." She then went up the stairs and left him to decide. The first day he screamed loud and long before he came up. But she worked hard to stay calm and let him wail for a bit. When he paused for a breath between screams she gently reminded him, "You can come when you're ready." Each day the crying got less and, by the end of the week, the fussing and begging were completely gone and he came up happily on his own.

The best part was that she began to have a vision for helping him learn to make wise choices. She realized that with her new approach Eli was learning a lot. He learned that his behavior didn't control his mom's emotions anymore, and that it was lonely and boring fussing at the bottom of the stairs. He practiced the helpful skill of self-calming. He also learned that he was responsible for getting himself up the stairs and that life was much more enjoyable when he did so quickly.

Calm Down, Connect, Offer Choices

Sometimes parents offer choices in an angry, intimidating way. If kids feel backed into a corner, they are likely to resist, even if offered some choices. When I start an interaction by calming myself down and then connecting with my child briefly, it minimizes my child's inclination to either fight or emotionally withdraw. It also gets him into a frame of mind to make a decision when I offer some reasonable choices.

The need to come up with two appropriate choices shifts the parent's brain out of a highly reactive mode into a more rational thinking state, and the need to evaluate each option and make a choice does the same for a child who is feeling out of control. These choices can simply be two possible ways to solve the conflict with my child that I can live with as a parent but that are not harsh or punitive.

Don attended one of our classes a year ago at his wife's request. He recently emailed us an account of the "aha" parenting moment he had as a result:

> *Every Friday in my son's classroom is Sharing Day when each kid can bring in a favorite toy or stuffed animal, etc., to show the class. On this particular day Cameron grabbed his hockey stick to take to school. I said firmly, "Cameron, I don't want you to bring your stick. Go pick out another toy to bring." I tried to explain that it might hurt someone, but he had already started to wail and throw a fit. I decided to try your advice from the class I had just attended. So I closed my eyes, took a deep breath, got down on my knees, looked him in his eyes and told him I loved him. He stopped wailing and kind of looked at me, so I knew I had his attention. I then explained he had two choices. Choice number one was he could leave the stick, pick out another toy, and then he could play with his stick the minute he got home from school. Choice number two was that he could leave the stick with me and not bring a sharing toy today.*
>
> *To my surprise it worked great. He stopped crying and went and put his stick away and grabbed another toy. He was not real happy with me, but we were then able to talk about why it was not a good idea to bring a hockey stick to a school classroom with 25 other kids.*
>
> *The long-term effect on that single moment has been re-*

markable. In this last year not only does Cameron listen better, but my wife and I are now much more aware of how we communicate with both our son and daughter. I've also become more aware of his perspective. Looking back, I understood that all Cameron wanted was to bring his favorite toy and share it with his friends. This was a pivotal incident for me through which I learned that parenting is not about forcing my will on our children but instead giving them choices so they can be successful.

Compliance vs. Biblical Obedience

Parents love this verse, and quote it often, "Children, obey your parents in the Lord, for this is right. Honor your father and mother – which is the first commandment with a promise – that it may go well with you and that you may enjoy long life on the earth" (Eph. 6:1–3).

But there's a problem with that—it is not written to us, it's written to our kids. It is intended to encourage children in the wonderful fruit of an honoring relationship with their parents. Notice that it does not say, "Parents, get your children to obey you, immediately, every time." It is certainly not intended as a way to coerce children into doing whatever a parent wants them to do.

Parents get their own verse immediately following the children's verse, (Ephesians 6:4) and it says "…do not exasperate your children; instead, bring them up in the training and instruction of the Lord." Parents who take their commandment to train and instruct seriously can put their focus on modeling obedience to the Lord and other authorities; teaching, encouraging, and affirming their children's obedience; and calmly following through with reasonable consequences as needed.

Ray was struggling to parent his intense 12-year-old son. He said his dad had frequently quoted the verse about children's obedience as he harshly disciplined Ray, who now years later was struggling to break out of that same habit of harsh, reactive discipline with his own son. Ray's eyes opened wide when he heard the parents' command to train and instruct instead of exasperate children. "I wish someone had told my dad that verse!"

We have seen much "sour fruit" in children whose parents put this premium on obedience because of their own need for control, looking good in front of others, and keeping life smooth. Although obedience is certainly an important quality to work toward, many parents are preoccupied with this one issue, while neglecting the importance of wisdom, compassion, faith, service, purity, etc. Parents frequently ask us, "How do I teach my child obedience?" but rarely ask about teaching other character qualities, or how to keep from exasperating their children.

In this preoccupation with obedience, many parents have also mistaken compliance for obedience. They work hard to get kids to comply but fail to nurture a true heart of obedience. Doing something out of fear of punishment is only outward compliance, unrelated to a heart attitude, and God has never been impressed by external behaviors without a sincere heart. "These people... honor me with their lips, but their hearts are far from me. Their worship of me is made up only of rules taught by men" (Isaiah 29:13).

Control though intimidation negates the biblical foundation of love for obedience and prepares our children to blindly obey other intimidating people once they leave our care. Children raised in controlling, authoritarian homes also have difficulty believing that God loves them and that it is safe and desirable to be intimate with him. Jana is a great example of this.

Jana was raised in a strong, faith-based home. Her parents loved her deeply and gave her an invaluable foundation of faith. But they resisted giving her choices and controlled her decisions in an effort to teach her absolute and quick obedience. Any delayed or noncompliant response on her part resulted in a spanking. Although generally compliant as a teenager, mistakes and disobedience were a big deal and she was easily ashamed and discouraged when she messed up. As is fairly typical of children raised without the freedom to question authority or make choices, though appearances would have suggested otherwise, Jana had not learned true obedience. When she left home at 18 she rebelled against all the years of control. She had no skills at making wise decisions, was desperate to please others and "obeyed" what her boyfriends told her to do. Of course it wasn't long before her choices had very painful consequences, the most substantial of which will follow her all her life.

> When children feel safe with us and believe that we are truly parenting for their benefit and not ours, they are much more likely to trust us and choose to obey.

True biblical obedience is a natural choice that flows from love and trust, not control. This trust believes that God's commands are truly beneficial and, even if difficult, they are a wise way to live. In Matthew 22:34–40 Jesus stated that all of God's specific commandments depended upon the primary commandments to love God and love others. This passionate love and loyalty that God desires draws his children to want to obey, even if it is confusing or difficult to do so. When children feel safe with us and believe that we are truly parenting for their benefit and not ours, they are much more likely to trust us and choose to obey for the right reasons or willingly accept our consequences when they disobey.

This is not at all about soft, let-'em-run-the-show parenting. This is about parenting with an insightful eye for my own selfishness and need for control, grace to give my child choices when possible, and a determination to get to the root of the issue if my child is truly defiant. True godly authority is resolved to follow through peacefully with respectful, helpful consequences.

For a strong-willed child, obedience may initially mean the child respectfully selects one of the choices offered. Parents set the boundaries and children function within them. This story from a missionary mom raising an extremely bright, intense daughter is a great example of perseverance and Godly authority. It also illustrates the long-term fruit of mentoring a stubborn child toward responsible independence and heart-felt obedience. It is a stark contrast to Jana's story above.

> *Our daughter, Andrea, seemed to be born wanting her own way. We tried just forcing our will on her, but every little thing became a major conflict. She didn't like to be told what to do, but her life seemed to be filled with orders: put on your clothes, please; brush your teeth; time to get into the car and go..., etc. Just getting her to put her shoes on to leave the house was a major issue. We couldn't avoid asking her to do things, so life became a miserable struggle of the wills.*

> *This struggle helped us to see vividly that God had created her as a strong person with a will of her own. We didn't want to punish her into compliance but we needed to find a way to have peace in our home while maintaining her inner strength. What we discovered was that by simply giving her options to choose*

from, we allowed her to use her intelligence and strength while not creating a conflict a hundred times a day. So instead of telling her to put on her shoes, she could choose to put her shoes on now or when we were ready to get out of the car at our destination. She was given the option to play outside with sun block on or she could stay under the umbrella without sun block.

We felt good about this approach since when God "parents" us he does not force us into submission but lets us know that we will reap what our choices sow (Galatians 6:7). It sounds simple, but the constant effort to think of reasonable options and consequences was exhausting. Every option for her had to be realistic and fair.

I remember one particular day when Andrea was about five; I was so tired of thinking up realistic choice options that I just asked her to cooperate—and, of course, she simply refused. I sat with her on the stairwell and just about cried. I pleaded with her to obey me just once because I asked her instead of having to think up choices and consequences. She quietly pondered my request and sweetly looked at me and said, "What will happen if I don't?" I just laughed. Once I explained what her consequence would be for not cooperating, she made a wise choice.

With all our battles with her as a little child, we worried we would have trouble in her teen years. We didn't. That's when we really saw the fruit of our efforts. Over time it became clear that Andrea felt responsible for her own life. She learned both by the fruit of making wise choices and the consequences of her bad choices. Sometimes it was so hard to follow through when she made a poor choice, but it was essential in keeping our authority with her. During her elementary school years she gradually began to do things simply because we asked her to, learning true *heartfelt obedience instead of forced compliance. Our relationship with her grew stronger, and she grew more and more responsible to make wise choices in her life.*

She is now a delightful and very responsible young woman enrolled in a Christian college. She has turned her God-given intelligence into a 4.0 grade point average. What we could have easily called an ability to "manipulate," she now uses to influence and lead as a Bible-study leader with her peers. We couldn't be prouder of her.

Chapter 14

Building a Child's Ability to Self-Correct Their Misbehavior

"What can we do to keep this from happening again?" It's a great question to ask to help avoid digging deeper and deeper "ruts" of misbehavior. But during the heat of a discipline moment is *not* the time to answer it. When upset, kids get easily overloaded, and to their stressed out young brains, we might as well be speaking Mandarin Chinese. Problem-solving attempts to avoid future similar misbehavior at best sound like a "blah,

> With a calm, even playful tone, you can constructively talk through conflicts by keeping a few simple goals in mind.

blah, blah" lecture, or a verbal attack. At worst, a parent's lectures about what needs to change in the future can escalate the situation, solve nothing, and may actually "fertilize" the misbehavior by giving intense attention to it.

Enlisting Kids' Ownership in Problem-solving Change

Asking the same question, "what can we do to keep this from happening again?" during "peacetime" is the best time to revisit the interaction and figure out how to do things differently. With a calm, even playful tone, you can constructively talk through conflicts by keeping a few simple goals in mind.

First, ask questions to help your kids identify their feelings and thoughts. Here are some great open-ended questions that tend to help kids learn to work through conflict and feel joined and understood rather than accused and judged. When they feel understood they are far more open to working collaboratively to solve past conflicts and prevent future problems.

- "How would you describe what happened?"
- "What was the most frustrating part for you?"
- "What do you wish you had done differently?"
- "What are your ideas for avoiding this kind of problem in the future?"

Let the kids answer, even if their perspectives are different than yours. Avoid questions answered with only "yes" or "no," or questions that might make the kids feel trapped. Questions like, "What were you thinking?" Or, "Did you think about what the other person was feeling?" tend to feel attacking and will lead to closed ended conversations because they feel accusing rather than truly curious.

Then, when you've heard from your kids, respectfully share your perspective and answers to the questions too. If the perspectives vary greatly, DO NOT simply tell the kids they are wrong. Instead validate their perspectives and acknowledge that the way everyone sees it is quite different. Work toward future solutions that you can agree on rather than past blame. This will gain your child's respect.

Once each person's thoughts and concerns are on the table, you can brainstorm possible solutions. Work with your kids to establish common goals such as: having fun at bedtime instead of fighting, developing a fair system for sharing chores, getting homework done most nights in time to play a game together, etc.

This process strengthens a message of "You are capable" (of wise behavior). Children gain confidence and skills when they can articulate their concerns respectfully and reach a creative solution or mutually acceptable compromise with a parent. For more details on collaborative problem-solving with your child, *The Explosive Child,* by Ross Greene, or www.livesinthebalance.org are great resources.

Dave and Nadine had frequent conflicts with Austin, their 11-year-old son about simply taking a shower. This issue had been a battleground for years, escalating to disrespect and defiance because Austin seemed determined to avoid hygiene tasks in general, and showering in particular. His parents were sick of it. Nothing had worked. Reasoning, bargaining and cajoling exhausted Dave and Nadine. Consequences exasperated Austin because he felt unfairly controlled and punished.

When they sat down as a family to discuss this problem, they all wanted to find a mutually agreeable solution that would help Austin feel responsible instead of nagged, and keep them all from getting so angry at each other. Dave and Nadine first listened carefully to all the things Austin disliked about taking a shower. Then they asked him how often he thought he should take a shower. His answer was predictable. "Once a week." Dave and Nadine countered with their ideal—two showers a day. They gave examples of why Dave often took two showers a day, and why pre-teen boys need to shower more frequently than in previous years. Because Austin had felt listened to, he listened to the logic in their perspective. He countered with twice a week, they countered with once a day, and then Austin finally suggested every other day, which was the minimum that his parents felt they could accept as a compromise. Because it was Austin's suggestion he felt good about it, and he now showers every other day, no complaints. Dave and Nadine are thrilled.

Proactively Building Skills

Another way to communicate the message of "You are capable" (of wise behavior) is to proactively help children learn to self-correct the misbehavior in the first place. One of the reasons children misbehave is that they don't have the skills to do otherwise, especially if stressed. These stressed children will not learn to self-correct without positive, proactive teaching and training when they are not misbehaving. For example, a child who frequently over-reacts by quickly getting angry or aggressive may have impulses he can't control. Instead of just giving consequences when he struggles to control himself, his parents can proactively teach him skills to better anticipate and think his way through his actions. Here are three skills that will help him avoid misbehavior, and how you could teach them.

- Make a plan: Help a child "get out of the immediate moment" and think ahead to plan his actions or activities. Outside the context of transitions, ask frequent questions that make him stop and think. "What's your plan about that?" "How will you accomplish that?" Even asking "What do you need to do to be ready to leave?" is more helpful than just, "Get your shoes and jacket on." These questions all engage his brain in the problem solving process rather than a "just do it" command and control process. As he gets accustomed to the process when he does not feel stressed by demands, he will grow more able to think his way through tougher and tougher transitions.

- Engage his thinking about consequences: "Hmm. What do you think will happen if...?" This is a great question to ask frequently about any of the choices your child might make. You can even talk about the impact of the choices of characters in a story or movie. Affirm his insights. Persisting at this through the ebbs and flows of non-stressful, every day life will help him to learn to weigh his options instead of reacting without thinking.

- Teach him to wait: Your child also can learn to wait for things appropriately as you intentionally delay granting his request for a few seconds or a few minutes. Add a little encouragement (i.e. a smile or thumbs up) while he's waiting, provide the desired item or action before the child gets to the brink of a meltdown, and then compliment his grown-up waiting. Also, help him learn to save up for things he wants instead of putting the item in the cart to stop his tantrum. In general, keep an eye out for any instances in which he uses self-control or delays gratification, and encourage him in his success.

Working to build skills to offset impulsiveness is just one example. The possibilities for strengthening kids to help them avoid misbehavior are endless. When parents use misbehaviors as insight to proactively guide a child's growth, children become more encouraged and parenting becomes more fun. It's like the difference between pulling weeds and planting flowers. Our first book, *How to Grow a Connected Family with Contagious Love and Faith,* focuses on how to proactively nurture children's character and skills in order for them to walk in the purposes for which they were created. Parents can also find other helpful resources on our website at www.connectedfamilies.org, including the free T.E.A.C.H. worksheet download, which guides parents in strategies for strengthening skills and values.

Strengthening our children to avoid misbehavior, instead of just waiting to give consequences when they mess up, strongly communicates, "I am for you, not against you." After the "No" of discipline, it's the "Yes." After the "Stop" it's the "Go" to help my child get back on a path of wise behavior. In the final section of the book, "Wisdom for Specific Challenges" we will include specific ideas related to each topic to proactively build the values and skills children need to avoid that particular misbehavior.

SECTION FOUR: "YOU ARE RESPONSIBLE... FOR YOUR ACTIONS"

Chapter 15

No Single "Right" Consequence

"So how does this work when, no matter what you've done to get your seven-year-old kid to put her shoes on, she keeps going outside with socks but no shoes? She must have wrecked 10 pairs of socks already this spring." This question was asked in a classroom filled with parents following one of our "Discipline that Connects" presentations: "Great question," I responded. "Who knows the right answer?" No hands went up.

Parents desperately long for the one right answer to solve their discipline issues. But in the light of all the various complexities, conditions, and nuances of each parent/child relationship, there is no consistent, satme-consequence-every-time right answer.

This question about socks gave us an opportunity to illustrate what a creative adventure it can be to put these principles in place and then try a consequence that helps our child learn to take responsibility. So I said to those at the workshop, "Around your tables, assume you've prepared your heart well. Assume you've let your child know she's loved despite this behavior. Assume you are helping her know that she's capable. What consequences might you put in place to help the little gal begin to take better responsibility for her socks? Make a list and then decide which answers are your table's favorites."

The group spent the next few minutes in energized conversation. Here are some of the consequences they listed:

- Have the girl go to her piggy bank and get money out to pay for ruined socks each time she ruins a pair, or have her pay for more at the next store visit.

- Put her in a time-out chair and stay with her until she has put her shoes on, explaining that she can't go outside without shoes on.
- Teach her to do the laundry and have her help with laundry each time she dirties her socks.
- Put all her wrecked socks in a box to show her when she runs out of socks. Then ask her what she wants to do. Use the opportunity to teach her about money, socks, and about honoring the resources and possessions God has provided.
- Take away my kids' socks until they are motivated to have socks. Then we'll figure out how they can be more responsible with them—maybe they buy their own socks.

These are all good examples of thoughtful consequences that may help children learn to be more responsible when they disobey about shoes and socks. Some may seem fitting for you and your kids, and others may not; you ultimately know best. What became really clear that day is that when parents take the time to think a bit, there are numerous constructive possibilities for discipline that can help children begin to take the reins of responsibility for their own lives. As parents learn to take the time to think think this way, they can test various consequences and stay calmer and well-connected to their kids.

And that's what the next chapter is about: learning as parents to think through effective consequences that really help children begin to understand that ultimately they are responsible for themselves and their actions.

Chapter 16

Natural Consequences: Children Reap What They Sow

The most powerful types of consequences parents have at their disposal are natural consequences. Galatians 6:7 says, "Do not be deceived: God cannot be mocked. A man reaps what he sows." This simply means that "If you do bad things, bad stuff naturally happens." But, "If you do good stuff, you will reap a harvest if you do not give up." Parents sometimes forget this important spiritual law when it's time to discipline. We tend to rush past or altogether forget about God's ready-made natural consequences to impose our own consequences. This may give us a feeling of power and control, but if we ignore the natural consequences of their behavior, we may well be blocking our children's learning. This was highlighted when a parent once approached us after a workshop and described this situation:

"I was working in the kitchen while listening to my children play in the next room. Things were going well until I heard my three-year-old daughter wailing the kind of wail that could only have been caused by my four-year-old son's aggression. I rinsed my hands and rounded the corner to see my son leaning over to pick her up. It looked like he had shoved her to the floor. But by the time I reached them, he was hugging her and telling her he was sorry." Her voice became stern "So what should the consequences be for pushing her down?"

Here is a parent's dream come true: A child demonstrating sincere remorse by comforting the little sister he has just hurt. The natural consequences (her pain, his remorse, and his desire to repair the relationship) had played out beautifully. But based on the mom's tone in asking the question, it seemed quite clear that if she had seen it happen and had been able to respond sooner, she would have stepped in, scolded her son, and removed the powerful moment of the son's self-motivated restoration. If she had intervened, instead of experiencing his sister's pain and sadness and his remorse, the son would have immediately focused on his mom's anger and his fear of her. If Mom had taken over, the opportunity for him to initiate reconciliation based on his own feelings of guilt would have been complicated at best, and lost altogether at worst.

> All too frequently parents jump in and start punishing or dealing with misbehavior before the children get to feel or experience the impact, or natural consequences, of their actions.

Two things are needed to help kids learn from natural consequences. The first, as demonstrated in the above story, is simply for parents to get out of the way and let it happen! All too frequently parents jump in and start punishing or dealing with misbehavior before the children get to feel or experience the impact, or natural consequences, of their actions. Sometimes parents even protect their kids from these consequences, such as when kids forget their lunch on the table. What are we inclined to do? Bring them the lunch, of course. By doing this we prevent our kids from experiencing the natural outcome of forgetting lunch. Which child is more likely to learn to remember lunch, the one whose parent brings the lunch or the one who goes hungry? It can be hard to let our kids "face the music" of their choices, but it helps them learn.

The second thing that is needed for kids to learn is to make sure they understand the natural consequences by explaining what they are. In the example of the little boy and his sister, it could have increased the son's learning if Mom had responded by saying, "I can see you feel bad about what happened to your sister. And it looks like she felt bad too. That's what happens when big brothers hurt little sisters. I can also see you want to comfort her and take care of her. That is why God made you her big brother. Doesn't it feel good to take care of her that way?" This kind of response can help motivate the son to care even better for his sister in the future. It truly does feel good to do something right.

Another way to explore natural consequences is simply to ask questions that help a child to discover the natural consequences for themselves. For example, you could ask, "What happens when brothers push their sister?"

Our daycare provider, Teri, shared with me (Lynne) her experience of helping our son Daniel understand the natural consequences of his behavior. One day Daniel was playing carelessly with a ball near Teri's glass-front cabinet. Teri brought him over to the cabinet, tapped on the glass gently and explained how it breaks into sharp pieces when things hit it. She asked him, "What might happen if kids play near the cabinet with a ball?" "It might break," he exclaimed. "That's right. Where do you think would be a good place to play with a ball?" "Over there on the other side." Daniel felt trusted to make a wise choice, and he played appropriately with the ball from then on.

This was a bit of an epiphany for me. It was so simple, but it had never occurred to me to do anything other than tell him what the rule was about where to play and what the consequence would be if he broke it. On a "good parenting day" I might have remembered to explain the reason for the rule. At times a "state-the-rule, rationale, and consequence" approach is perfectly appropriate, but Teri saw that this was a great opportunity to teach wisdom, self-control and respect instead of just compliance.

Other common natural consequences might be:

- **When a child wrecks socks:** You have ruined your socks and now there are no more socks to wear. Your feet are dirty because your socks had holes, and if you come inside you will dirty the carpet.
- **When a sister hits her brother:** The brother's body gets hurt and his feelings get hurt. He might not want to play with her anymore. The sister may feel sad.
- **When a child interrupts:** It's hard for people to talk; they get frustrated with him. They may not want to be with him much.
- **When a child grabs a toy:** The other child's feelings get hurt. He may grab one back. The toy might get broken if they fight over it.
- **When children leave messes:** Other people can trip over the things or feel disrespected because they don't like the clutter. It can be hard to find things.
- **When a child doesn't do his homework:** She (not her parents) gets a bad grade and gets farther behind in class. It's hard for the teacher when some students don't keep up with the class. The child doesn't learn the study skills that will help her later. She feels bad about her grades (whether or not she'll admit it).
- **When a child steals:** The person she steals from loses what belongs to him, something he may have worked hard for. He may become angry or worried. The child who stole may feel guilty.
- **When a child is verbally abusive/disrespectful:** There is

a break/disconnect in the relationship because of the hurt feelings. The receiver of the mean words may avoid the relationship or try to get revenge later. The hurt person may believe untrue things about herself that hurts how she relates to others.

- **When a child lies:** Trust is broken. There are yucky, guilty feelings (knot in stomach). The child's heart grows hard if no one finds out. The person lied to doesn't want a liar for a friend.

Learning to talk about natural consequences in a relaxed non-judgmental way equips our children to take more honoring responsibility for their behavior. A simple example of this occurred when I (Jim) was leading a group of high-risk teens on a wilderness trip.

I had all but given up trying to get the teens to quit using foul language. After all, it was normal language for them and I didn't think it a high priority in light of the various troubled homes these kids had come from. But our guide, Kathy, thought otherwise. After only a few minutes with them, listening to all kinds of cussing and cursing to which she was not accustomed, Kathy gathered the group. "I can see you youngsters have a lot of energy and a vocabulary that is quite colorful. Now I can't control the words you use, but I figure if you're going to be using them, you should know how they affect me." She smiled slightly and continued. "The words you use, particularly the words that curse the God and the Jesus I love, cause my spirit to hurt. So I will greatly appreciate it if you decide to stop using those words and chose words that could be used in a G-rated movie." She paused and the youth sat in silence, the impact of Kathy's description of natural consequences sinking in. "Thanks for listening."

I could see how Kathy beautifully spoke only of the natural consequences of the group's word selection, both on the negative and the positive side. "The words you use… cause my spirit to hurt"—a natural consequence. "I will greatly appreciate it if you decide to stop." These are natural consequences, spoken almost as an invitation.

I've spent most of my life in some sort of work with high-risk teens, and to this day I have never seen a more effective way to help kids take responsibility without imposing any sort of consequence. Simply by her respectful gathering and her sharing of the natural consequences of language use, Kathy motivated the youth to do better. From that moment, and throughout the five-day trip, the teens worked hard to use the language Kathy requested. And when they slipped, they apologized. They truly owned the responsibility for their language.

Of course parents will not always find such gracious ways to help their kids understand natural consequences and, even if they do, kids may not always respond so well. But knowing that imposed consequences will be the next step may motivate kids to try to understand and take responsibility for the natural consequences of their actions. Before leaping right to imposed consequences, parents can help motivate their school-aged and older kids by saying, "We might be able to avoid a consequence if it's clear that you learned from your mistake and have a plan about keeping it from happening again. What was the impact on everybody involved, including you? What could you do to resolve the situation for everyone? Would you like to talk about it with me?"

The Natural Consequences of Effective Use of Natural Consequences

If parents are diligent in sowing the seeds of effective teaching about natural consequences, they will reap a harvest of the following outcomes:

- Children will feel bad about what they should feel bad about instead of bad about the way Mom or Dad treated them.
- They will become increasingly internally motivated.
- Children will be ready to take responsibility for their own lives when the time comes.
- Talking about positive and negative natural consequences of different choices strengthens judgment as a child learns to consider past actions and future results.
- Understanding the emotions that naturally occur in interactions or conflict builds your child's social skills and compassion and can actually lead to connection, even when kids have misbehaved.
- Even if an imposed consequence is also necessary for your child, understanding the natural impact of his behavior helps a child see the purpose of the imposed consequence.

This approach may open the door to having your children take responsibility for their actions without needing to impose any further consequences. But for most kids, having a sound strategy for imposed consequences is also needed to help them take responsibility for their actions and learn the deeper message that they are responsible for their lives.

Chapter 17

Thinking Biblically about Consequences

"If you talk to me that way again you're grounded for a month!" We've all probably said something like that in a desperate moment, but it's typical of two common problems with the way parents impose consequences. The first is when parents are impulsive or reactive and give random and harshly delivered consequences. They are not thoughtful about biblical approaches and lack vision about what well-administered discipline might produce. It's a quick-fix approach that is fueled by the second problem, which is a belief that if the consequence is painful enough the behavior will stop. This perspective leads some parents to simply take away whatever the child loves most as their standard punishment.

Combine these two problems and you have impulsive and angry parents doling out various "painful" punishments with little to no long-term effectiveness in reaching the hearts of their children. Here are more examples of how it might sound:

- "If you don't get off that computer right now you'll be in your room the rest of the night."
- "That's the last straw. It's time for a spanking."
- "If you don't eat those vegetables you're going to the time-out chair."
- "You are not getting away with treating your sister like that. No video games for you this weekend."
- "I've had it! You are done using my car!"

The list goes on. The point is that while the above consequences might actually help a child learn to take responsibility, the way they are delivered (quick, harsh, painful) prevents the learning. This common approach is convenient, doesn't take a lot of thought and sometimes can be effective in the short run. But there are pitfalls to the approach:

1. If your child is overly focused on something and you frequently take it away, it will tend to increase his obsession as he defends his right to it.
2. Your child will probably resent what she perceives as your unfair control, which decreases your actual influence with her over time.
3. Valuable learning opportunities are lost. Your child may simply learn to get sneakier, because he is not learning to desire wise behavior for good reasons.

When parents think more carefully about the consequences they use, they can become less reactionary and harsh about discipline and more peaceful and purposeful. So what are effective, biblical consequences? The nature of "biblical consequences" is a hotly disputed topic among Christians. God's discipline of his misbehaving children can give us helpful, practical insight into the use of imposed consequences. God was amazingly insightful, purposeful, and creative in the consequences he used. As I seek to follow his example, I am inspired by a new vision for discipline. Here are a few examples of discipline principles and consequences from the Scriptures.

Do-over/Practice a right response: When Jonah refused to go to Ninevah, he got a little help (transportation) and a second chance to do what he was told to do. When Jesus dealt with prostitutes, tax collectors, and other "assorted sinners," he often short-circuited any impending punishment and instead exhorted them with some form of "go and sin no more." When his disciples argued over who was the greatest, he put a little child in their midst as an example and exhorted them to be simple, humble servants.

Perhaps the most powerful example is Christ's response to Peter. In Christ's greatest hour of need, Peter lied three times and denied that he knew him. Instead of

> When parents think more carefully about the consequences they use, they can become less reactionary and harsh about discipline and more peaceful and purposeful.

discipline or rebuke for the lies, Jesus set Peter up to tell the truth—three times! "Do you love me?" Peter passionately, honestly answers "Yes!" At the heart of the question is a vision, not an indictment. I can just imagine Jesus, with a knowing smile, thinking, "This Peter is the very kind of strong-willed, bold, and passionate guy we need to jump-start the church. Father, how might I help him walk in the good works you prepared him to do?" Each time that Peter answered "Yes," Jesus pronounced, "Then feed my sheep!"—which Peter went on to do with great passion and conviction as one called by God to ignite the early church. Simple applications of this idea of do-over/practice a right response might look like this:

If a child whines loudly to get more food, giving the opportunity to practice asking two or three times respectfully can help him learn to ask more respectfully in the future. Or if a child

JIM & LYNNE JACKSON

leaves on lights at night, he can be required to go around the house under supervision a couple of times and turn off the lights.

Lose the privilege: Adam and Eve lost the privilege of life in the garden because of their sin. When Moses dishonored God in front of the Israelites he lost the privilege of leading them into the Promised Land and all the faithless adults also lost the privilege of going. A prophet told King Jehoshaphat, "Because you have made an alliance with Ahaziah [an evil king], the LORD will destroy what you have made." The ships were wrecked and were not able to set sail to trade (2 Chron. 20:37). God also took the son conceived by the adulterous union of David with Bathsheba.

In light of this scriptural principle, it is fitting to remove privileges from our kids when they misuse them. Whether a four year-old with Matchbox cars or a seventeen-year-old with the family car, if the car isn't used according to clearly stated expectations, it is reasonable to take away the car until restitution is made. If a child is disrespectfully demanding, parents can calmly state, "You've lost the privilege of asking for this today. I'll bet you'll do really well tomorrow when you try again."

Make restitution/reconcile: Reconciliation is the very heartbeat of the gospel, but somehow it is often missed in parents' discipline. Is it any wonder that there is so much unresolved conflict and division within the church? Many of us were not taught to make restitution or reconcile conflicts as children. Matthew 18 begins, "If your brother sins against you..." but it does not continue, "tattle to the church leaders and get them to punish him." The scripture requires three attempts to reconcile, with gradually increasing assistance in the process, before church discipline is utilized for a defiant offender.

Practically speaking, when kids offend or hurt others, they can be required to make restitution before getting other social privileges.

These ideas—do-over/practice a right response, lose the privilege, and make restitution/reconcile—are types of consequences that go beyond punishment when kids are off track. These truly help them to get back on track.

Spanking

Many parents ask about the value of spanking. There are certainly references in the Bible about the use of the rod and about chastising. Christian leaders take vastly different positions on the interpretations of these references. On one side of the spectrum these leaders promote the loving use of "the rod," or spanking, as a primary tool for disobedience and defiance of all kinds. On the other side, leaders suggest that Jesus ushered in a nonviolent approach to life and parenting and that any references to corporal punishment are figurative, encouraging parents to be strong in their authority without inflicting physical pain.

We are not dogmatic about whether or how to use spanking as a form of biblical discipline. We are quite dogmatic about a parent's responsibility to be growing in grace and truth for parenting and in discernment about what consequences effectively reach the hearts of their children.

What we know for certain, as we look at the Scriptures, is that God occasionally used strong physical consequences for sin. He afflicted King Azariah with leprosy because he did not eliminate places of idol worship. Ananias and Saphira lost their lives due to deception and disobedience. However, physical punishment seems to be the exception compared to the frequency of other types of natural and imposed consequences that the Lord used to discipline his children, especially when dealing with an individual person.

With that in mind, we believe that spanking can be one tool for effective discipline of some children, in some situations, and by some parents. We do not believe it is a scriptural mandate for discipline. We believe the use of the word "rod" in Proverbs is as much or more about proper use of authority as it is about physical punishment. What we conclude, as we look closely at this issue scripturally, is that it is up to us to parent wisely and to trust the Holy Spirit for guidance about how or if to employ spanking.

Keep in mind that there are some children who will always misunderstand a spanking. Many highly-sensitive children, regardless of the nature of the parents' approach to it, will perceive spanking as a traumatizing, humiliating experience. When we utilized spanking we were very careful about it, but no matter how wisely or calmly we spanked, our sensory-sensitive daughter, Bethany, was traumatized by the experience and our strong-willed Daniel was altogether defiant, with an expression that said, "I will get even for this injustice." Both children, now vibrant Christ-followers, look back on the experience as confusing and counterproductive. They say that only when our consequences were more directly associated with their misbehavior did they feel respect for us and begin to develop internal motivation to go and "sin no more." The few times that Noah was spanked, he seemed to respond fairly well. But we hardly ever spanked Noah because by the time he came along as our third child we had become wiser to develop more learning-oriented consequences.

The problem we see with spanking, and we see it a lot, is that spanking is the primary discipline tool in the toolbox for parents who are not themselves disciplined in the art of effective discipline. This probably explains why, although the research is varied on spanking, it usually appears to be counterproductive, increasing a child's tendencies toward aggression.

For some parents, and for some kids, spanking may be an effective way to address misbehavior and open the child's heart to deeper teaching and a more connected relationship. If a parent's spanking of his child is not leading to these outcomes, then he should stop spanking and think more creatively about related consequences and ways to proactively help the child. We are to be prayerful, discerning and paying attention to each discipline experience, applying what we learn as we seek consequences that truly help children take more responsibility for their lives.

Understand *Why* Your Child is Misbehaving

Neither a surgeon nor a car mechanic tries to fix a problem when he or she doesn't know the cause. Likewise, my discipline ought to give great consideration to the various underlying causes of misbehavior. It seems that the many unique reasons children misbehave can be grouped into three main categories.

1. A negative identity

Children who struggle to control their behavior are often discouraged or anxious. If they frequently misbehave, they may have developed an identity as a troublemaker, whiner, angry child, selfish kid, black sheep in the family, etc. Their template says, "This is the kind of kid I am so this is how I respond in this kind of situation." Certainly self-perceptions can fluctuate somewhat from day to day—we can all relate to feeling like a wise parent one day when everything goes smoothly and a failure the next—but, overall, we have predominant self-perceptions that are important factors in the behaviors we choose. As a growing child's misbehavior becomes more challenging, and the struggles between parent and child become more volatile, that child can begin to form entrenched negative identities that become a snowball of resentment, discouragement, and even despair.

It can be hard not to respond to a misbehaving child as a troublemaker and to instead respond in a way that reminds him of who he truly is: loved no matter what, called by God for special purposes, and capable of a wise response. This certainly doesn't mean I should give a theology lesson when I discipline my child, but it does mean that this perspective of who he or she was created to be is woven into our interactions. The need for children to grow a healthy, Christ-centered identity is the basis for the many practical, proactive strategies found in the appendix.

Consider some specific ways you may want to strengthen your child's identity, even in misbehavior, as someone who:

- is learning self-control
- is forgiven and loved
- enjoys serving others
- often makes wise choices
- loves his siblings despite the skirmishes
- has a heart to love God and others

After giving Daniel "reconciliation consequences" for an aggressive conflict, we would occasionally observe, "You seem a lot happier now than you did after you hit Bethany. That's because when you're kind to your sister you are living out of the true heart of love that God gave you for her. You can recognize it by the joy you feel." This approach helped him grow to value his role as a caring older brother.

The apostle Paul knew the importance of identity as a foundation for behavior. In all his epistles he strongly stated the believer's identity in Christ as the basis for how to live life. Even in his very confrontational letters to churches in sin, Paul started his letters with a statement of his calling by God to guide them. He then gave a blessing of grace and peace, and always included solid teaching about their identity in Christ. Likewise, we can respond from a God-given authority as parents to bless our children and teach them about their true identity when they misbehave. If the apostle Paul was adamant that behavioral change should flow from an identity anchored in faith, we ought to be mindful of this as soon as our children begin understanding simple faith concepts.

Authors Chip and Dan Heath, in their book Switch - How to Change Things When Change is Hard cite research that concludes, "Because identities are central to the way people make decisions, any change effort that violates someone's identity is likely doomed to failure." (p154) This principle leaves little doubt about why it's important for me to work at a heart level. I can remind my child of my love and God's love, encourage her and develop the skills she needs to succeed instead of simply trying to stop her difficult behavior.

I (Jim) coached Lila, a 19-year-old girl who was repeatedly making poor choices surrounding sex and alcohol use and feeling a great deal of shame about it. These choices were rooted in the firm belief (identity), "I have an addictive personality type and therefore I have no self-control." I told her that lots of people have addictive personality types, myself included, and it doesn't obligate her to the choices she felt stuck in. We discussed times when she had used good self-control and what enabled her to do that. We also talked about what gave her true joy. Her whole countenance changed as she talked about how much she loved to serve people. She left the session significantly encouraged, found a job as a server in a classy restaurant and began a long road toward better choices.

2. Perceived cost/reward

People also choose how they will act by simply weighing the cost/reward: "What benefit could I get out of doing this, or what might it cost me?" Children are much more likely to choose misbehavior if they get "rewarded" by lots of intense attention from Mom and Dad when they misbehave, and/or they feel powerful when they control their parent's emotions. (We can be very entertaining when we are out of control!) "Prepare my heart" tips will help parents stay calm in specific situations and avoid "fertilizing" their child's misbehaviors.

If a child doesn't see any good reason to behave well, why wouldn't he just default to misbehavior? I can help my child think through the natural consequences of his behavior, and/or impose logical consequences to help change his perception of the cost/reward of a particular action. If my child knows that if she whines for something she a) is practicing behavior that makes people want to avoid her, b) gets no intense attention for whining, and c) loses the possibility of getting that particular item that day, the whining certainly will diminish.

3. Physical (body/brain) factors

Sometimes a child misbehaves because his body is working against him (i.e., fatigue, low blood sugar, under-or over-stimulation, etc. Or he may simply lack the skills (a.k.a. neuropathways) to respond wisely and needs help in learning and practicing those skills.

Raul was an eight-year-old who struggled to focus, was always moving and making noise, and could erupt at fairly minimal provocation if he was over-stimulated or having a rough day. His parents, Jose and Bella, contacted us for coaching because he had been suspended from the church's Wednesday-night Bible program due to his out-of-control behavior and impulsive aggression toward other kids.

Raul was already experiencing a strong, logical consequence for his aggression by not getting to participate in Wednesday-night activities, so Jose and Bella put their focus on teaching and encouraging him. This started with helping Raul understand emotions—his own and other people's—and how his behavior made others feel. They talked through the impact of his aggression on others but also looked carefully for examples of kindness and gentleness and helped him feel good about the impact of his positive choices. They taught him how to tune in to his energy/anger level and use practical strategies to calm his body down. He also learned to plan out his actions more (telling his parents when and where he was going, how he would play with others), which decreased his impulsiveness.

Raul's parents and siblings noted numerous changes, but the highlight was when he announced, "I'll be fine going back to church on Wednesdays. I'm not an angry kid anymore." Clearly Raul's identity had changed in the process. Our final coaching sessions focused on channeling his energy and intensity into healthy leadership skills.

This was a great example of effective discipline, a total package of helpful consequences and training that gave the message, "You are *responsible* for your actions," given by parents who had *"prepared* their hearts" and communicated, "you are *loved*" and, "you are *capable.*"

SECTION FIVE: TWO FINAL IMPORTANT CHAPTERS

Chapter 18

What to Do When It All Falls Apart - The Power of Rebuilding

We hope by now that you're inspired and equipped to prepare your heart well, communicate love no matter what, recognize and affirm your child's capability, and impose consequences that truly grow a child's sense of responsibility. Having these principles clearly etched in your heart and mind will guide your vision for connecting with your child's heart when you discipline.

However, Lynne and I must confess, that even with this inspiration and concrete vision in place, and having learned numerous skills for engaging constructively with our children's misbehavior, we blew it. A lot. We reacted instead of responding thoughtfully through the lens of vision. We exerted our power in order to control. We disciplined for our comfort rather than in our kids' best interest. We made demands that had no sound basis, simply because "we're the parents." We were quite effective at disguising our selfish, sinful motives behind masks of authority, logic and even "spiritual" guidance. As a result, on numerous occasions we simply did not obey first part of the command in Ephesians 6:4. We "exasperated" our children. Our discipline methods "provoked them to anger" (see Eph. 6:4 in the NASB).

But we thank God that even when our parenting was out of alignment with his purposes, God was still present and active. We're grateful that the Lord established in our hearts and minds a vision for how we wanted to discipline, anchored in the Discipline the Connects principles. We worked hard to talk about these guiding ideas, with each other and our kids, and even write them down. The result of this hard work? When we blew it, we knew it, and we knew what to do about it. When we exasperated out kids, we were inspired and equipped to rebuild in a way that "unexasperated" them, and also honored the second part of Ephesians 6:4; to "bring them up in the training and instruction of the Lord." How? We compared our actions to our vision, recognized that they didn't line up, and then went back to confess and restore what we'd torn down.

When parents really blow it with a child and hurt the relationship, they often feel a mixture of guilt for their own actions and resentment of the kid's behavior. It's tempting to offer a quick "drive-by apology." Maybe mumbling something like, "Sorry I was kinda harsh." It's like slapping a little plaster on a crack—a temporary fix of a problem that will reemerge under stress. It may ease the guilt a bit, but does little to truly restore the relationship or prevent the problem from happening again. Instead, we can rebuild. Rebuilding brings our vision to life. It's in the messes of life, the crises, where our theology becomes real.

Let's go back to the day when I (Jim) came home to find my kids fighting over a magazine when I arrived home. I came in the door and yelled at them, making harsh demands dictated by my selfish desires. I did not prepare my heart before speaking and demanding. I communicated no love and angrily proclaimed, "You're being rude and disrespectful!" Between the lines of my spoken words was an unspoken message, "What's wrong with you?" My son's well learned response, "Where's the connection, Dad?" jarred me. So I asked for a "do-over."

As I returned to the garage it was easy to reflect on what just happened, and rebuild what I'd torn down, because I had a memorized and practiced set of simple principles to guide my thinking. I prepared my heart by praying. I re-entered and communicated love, "Hey kids, great to see you!" The kids settled down. I asked if they could solve this on their own or needed help, thus communicating a new unspoken message, "I believe in you and your capability to solve this on your own." I gave them the responsibility for solving it respectfully and asked them to take the conflict out of the main part of the house. What three minutes earlier had been torn down was now rebuilt, and all of us were more encouraged and aligned with the joy of the Lord.

Sometimes it takes longer. Lynne had a similar experience, but that took a little more work to bring to constructive conclusion.

Guests were coming, and we were all stressed from cleaning up our messy house. As one child took out frustration on the other, I (Lynne) grew irate with the aggressive behavior. I felt pressed for time and with commando zeal sent them both into one of the bedrooms with a scathing order to quickly resolve the conflict. My glare at the aggressor left no doubt as to the focus of my anger. As soon as they were alone, that child, fueled by my negative energy, fired a load of hurtful words at the other, resulting in an explosion of tears. I heard the scream and sobs, and realized that I had contributed significantly to the outcome. My example had been followed quite well by the aggressive child. This was a great rebuilding opportunity, except for the fact that I would soon need to cordially greet our guests. So I had to choose, my guests or my kids. I asked Jim to finish preparation and engage the guests.

I started with an apology. "Kids, I felt a bunch of pressure to be ready for guests, and I took my stress out on you. You didn't deserve that. I'm sorry, will you forgive me?" They settled down immediately and both nodded. I invited them to sit near me on the bed and put my arms around each of them, thus re-connecting. This quickly put me back in the position of trusted mentor instead of angry bully. I then enlisted their ideas about how to reconcile this, while adding my own perspective. It took longer than I'd have liked, but we left the room laughing and the children's relationships restored as they then apologized and forgave each other.

So you can see, what goes around comes around. And when we are intentional about rebuilding, what comes around more often than not is kids who follow our example.

These kind of results doesn't happen over night. It takes prayerful, humble persistence. It is in our humility that we will gain proper authority. By relentlessly going back to rebuild, parents will open the door of their children's hearts to the redemptive purposes of God to restore broken relationship.

> It is in our humility that we will gain proper authority.

When parents are willing to eat their own humble pie, and make a commitment to doing their part to rebuild, it prepares their kids to rebuild the damage in the relationship that they were responsible for. Based on how the rebuilding process unfolds, parents may even choose to revise punitive or hastily given consequences, in favor of setting kids up to make restitution for their hurtful or unwise choices.

Confess/Apologize "Therefore confess your sins to each other and pray for each other so that you may be healed..." (James 5:16)

Admit to your child that your actions and/or attitudes were not OK. This confession does not excuse what your child did, but it shows an example of a repentance. You might say something like this, "I know I was quite harsh and thoughtless with you. I'm sorry. I wish I had been more thoughtful." Then, before continuing into further re-building, ask for forgiveness.

This simple rebuilding step will likely set a much more constructive tone for further conversation about whatever happened. Whether a child is three, thirteen, or for that matter, thirty years old, a parent's contrite heart and apology can powerfully pave the way for restored relationship and a child's ensuing repentance.

Re-Connection - I prioritize the message of love

When a child has been harshly or firmly disciplined, that child tends to feel rejected, unwanted, and receives a message, "You are a problem." Counteracting this message is a simple as re-connecting. Whatever the behavior, even in appropriately firm discipline, kids need to know that they are loved. So say to them, "I know this is hard right now, but nothing you do can keep me from loving you." Then act on it. Spend time with them and do something fun; or hug them, rub their backs, and even pray with them, thanking God that his love never leaves us. Real love is not a reward or incentive for kids to behave well. That's not the point. The point is love freely given, as an example of God's unconditional love.

Engage and Enlist Your Child

When parents apologize it sets the stage to engage the child in the rebuilding process. An honest confession about what you've done and what you wish you had done opens the way to ask, "What did you do?" and, "What do you wish you had done?" Because you set an example, your child can now follow it. This doesn't make the rest of the conversation easy, but it opens the door.

Your child may be reluctant at first, or have a hard time putting words to his feelings. He may continue to grumble or complain. But once you have calmed down and started to rebuild by apologizing and re-connecting, even if your child is still defensive or resistant, you are back on track. As you are more purposeful and respectful toward your child, you will set a tone and take an approach that at some point will feel more inviting to your child.

From this place, instead of grand pronouncements, "You know better than that!" or, "How many times do I have to tell you?" you can be more ask helpful questions, "What were you hoping for?" or, "Tell me more about what you want." Your child will probably still not be on board with you. "What do you think I was hoping for? You NEVER pay attention!" This can be hard to hear. It can be easy, even natural, when you're working hard to rebuild, to get frustrated if your child answers like this. But this is what you can expect when they are hurt and upset, and it can provide a potent opportunity for you to model a new way of responding. Instead of, "How dare you!" you can continue with the goal of engaging and enlisting your child, and say with curious indifference, "I can see you're pretty frustrated with me. I don't blame you. I've been a bit of a heel. So it seems to you I never pay attention. Tell me more about that." Notice there are no judging statements. Just gracefully re-framing what you hear, and inviting more. If you persist in the new goal of engaging, your child will eventually begin to respond in new ways too.

You'll know the child is engaged in rebuilding when he starts to work with you instead of against you. With younger kids, the attitude and mood may just change as you feel safe to your child. He may all of a sudden listen and respond when before he was defensive. With older kids it will likely be a bit slower. Stay patient, and listen for subtle differences in responses and body language. She may say things like this, "I just feel so stupid" or, "I don't know what to do" or, "I wish I could figure it out." These statements suggest the child is now focusing on herself and the problem rather than on you and your energy about the misbehavior.

Once the child begins to engage, you can enlist him or her in the process of figuring out a better future (not assigning blame to the past). Questions to help this process might be, "How would you like to see this go if it happens again?" or, "What do you want me or you to do differently if this comes up again?" or, "What was the best thing we did to make this work out well?" Based on the answers given, you could even invite your child to practice a respectful response.

Finally, as you discuss consequences, invite the child to consider (if he is old enough, perhaps five or six) what consequence might really help him learn better behavior. If he gets stuck, offer options. For example, if your child angrily threw toys or got sassy about picking up before bed, say to him, "I really want to help you learn to clean up and be responsible in more respectful ways." Then ask, "What consequence do you think will help you learn?" He may or may not have ideas. If he does, listen and consider whether any might truly help him learn. If not you can offer, "I have some ideas. Do you want to hear them, or do you still want to think of your own?" List the consequences you've discussed. From those you are willing to enforce offer, "Which of these do you want to try?" Then let him choose and follow through.

Here's a real-life example of rebuilding at work, as told by Vicki, the mom of eight-year-old Haley.

> Haley was at a neighbor's house playing for much of the morning. When I went to get her she was very upset about leaving. I grew more stern as her objections grew more resistant. I don't know what exactly I said, but she finally relented, and be-

grudgingly followed me outside. On the short walk to our house Haley kept up her verbal assault and finally kicked me hard in the back of my legs, almost knocking me down. Haley is a very intense child, but this was new. I was furious and I let her know it! Our strong reactions to her intensity were backfiring more regularly lately, but my anger kept me from seeing my way clearly out of this one. So I called my husband and told him what happened, and insisted that he spank Haley. Josh was shocked and angry at what Haley had done. Because spanking often made matters worse with Haley, he didn't feel good about it, but he spanked her anyway. This threw Haley into a screaming, explosive tirade. We were at a loss. All we knew for sure that we didn't want this conflict to end this way. As we reflected on what we'd learned in coaching sessions we decided we needed to rebuild.

So Josh convinced Haley to go for a drive with him, just to connect through some car games and maybe talk a little. I took this time to pray and ponder what had happened, and how to rebuild. When Josh and Haley returned we gathered the family and I shared what I had learned from God's Word and through prayer regarding my own anger. I also apologized for those instances when I had reacted in anger to an issue and shared that with God's help, I was going to make an effort to really set anger aside in my parenting. I shared that I love each of my children very much, and that we are a family that loves each other and wants to encourage and build one another up using gentle words and loving actions. We affirmed that it is good that we are a family of grace and forgiveness.

We then asked Haley if she wanted to have a "do-over." We asked her what she could do differently when asked to stop doing something she enjoys. She gave her answer and we practiced responding that way. We clearly established that if she was disrespectful like this again she would lose the privilege of going to a friend's for a while. She had a real-life opportunity a few days later to go to a friend's house. We reminded her of the respectful response she had practiced and when we called her home she did very well. It seems our rebuilding approach opened her to our hearts of love and our teaching about respect. We have a long way to go, but this experience anchored our commitment to connecting and rebuilding well.

Chapter 19

Conclusion - Bill and Layna's Story

Bill and Layna were chasing the American dream. They both had good jobs; they lived in a nice house and had two elementary-aged kids and a dog. The kids were involved in typical things and doing well in school. They went to church on Sundays and got involved in a few things there. But typical troubles with their girls, and a slow growing negative energy in the household left Bill and Layna with a little ache in the back of their thinking, a little fear that, as Christians, they were missing God's mark for their family. So they signed up for a "Discipline that Connects" workshop at their church.

They learned the "Discipline that Connects" principles and felt convicted. After the workshop, Layna came to me and confessed in tears, "We have things totally backwards. We thought we were doing just fine but we've realized that we have no vision and have just taken our blessings for granted. We are leaving here changed people because we now feel God's sense of calling and purpose for parenting."

That was ten years ago. While the children and families around them kept growing up in fairly typical fashion, Bill and Layna's family started to change little by little as they did their best to practice the four main principles in this book. At first glance the family didn't look a whole lot different. But a closer look revealed some subtle but significant changes.

Instead of Disney World vacations or cruises like the neighbors took, they went on family mission trips for three years. Their oldest girl, Sydney, started a little business, getting donated old jeans, sewing them into cute little purses and selling them in order to raise money to build houses for Native Americans on their reservations. The youngest, Hannah, started saving allowance money so that she could give it away. While some of their peers started chasing boys at young ages and slowly fell into the various troubles that comprise our country's dire statistics, Sydney and Hannah stood apart. They were friends with boys, but never obsessed. They never experimented with drugs or alcohol. They grew to be self-confident, responsible, and faith-filled girls. In ninth grade, when peer relationships are the strongest, Sydney decided that God was leading her to switch schools because she recognized that the pressure she was feeling was not healthy. She went on to graduate from high school and is now well prepared and eager to be a light for Christ on her college campus. Her sister has made the same choice, to switch schools in order to grow in her faith and be well prepared for spiritual maturity beyond high school.

> Too many children raised in the church are walking away from biblical faith. There are many reasons for this, and we believe that the way kids are disciplined has much to do with it.

This family would say that they still have a long way to go. But they clearly changed their goals from the typical goals of fast solutions to behavioral problems and pursuit of the typical American dream. Instead, they pursued the goal of living out their growing faith in the everyday stuff of life, while disciplining through the lens of the "Discipline that Connects" principles. The result is that Sydney and Hannah are flourishing as young followers of Christ. This family was transformed because of their desire to live out the gospel in their home every day—even in their discipline. They are in a very small minority.

Too many children raised in the church are walking away from biblical faith. There are many reasons for this, and we believe that the way kids are disciplined has much to do with it. Children disciplined with quick-fix, controlling, and immediate behavior messages begin believing that they are a problem, that no matter what they do they can never measure up. They learn to view God's authority the same way they view their parents' authority. We frequently hear kids say things like, "My parents are killjoys." Or, "They just set me up to fail." Or, "No matter how hard I try I feel like I'm a big disappointment." When we ask kids about their view of God, they say the same things. It's pretty obvious where the view of God comes from. It comes from the way parents treat their kids, especially the way they treat their kids when the kids misbehave.

Sydney and Hannah, however, are concrete examples of what we consistently see when parents are committed to thoughtful, Christ-centered parenting. anchored by firm but graceful discipline.

Encouraged, Inspired and Equipped

We write so that parents will be encouraged, inspired, and equipped to dive into discipline challenges with a vision to connect with their child's heart—even during the toughest times. When the child's heart is connected to his parents, his heart will be much more open to connection with God and God's purposes. In the words of our friend Rob Reinow of Visionary Parenting, "The shortest distance between your child's heart and Christ is you."

With this in mind, we recognize that the way we discipline our children when they misbehave is perhaps our most powerful opportunity to show them what God's grace and truth are all about. So we extend this invitation: If you have not already done so, change the primary reason for disciplining your kids. Instead the goals of controlling, changing, or stopping misbehavior, make 'Discipline that Connects' your goal.

With this as your goal, you can now evaluate your discipline not just based on whether your child complied, because that compliance may be only temporary. Instead, you can evaluate based on how you prepared your heart, how you communicated love no matter what, and how you encouraged your child's capability and responsibility. You can then reflect on how God is at work to build character in both you and your child. You can also consider more than whether the consequences "worked" to change behavior, and instead consider— How did the consequences relate to the misbehavior? What is my child truly learning?

Where you have met your goals, you can be encouraged; where you have failed to meet your goals, you can confess and rebuild. Even when you meet your goals, you can be freed of the sense of responsibility for your children's choices, because it's not your job to try to control them.

As you lovingly guide your children to take responsibility for their own lives, they will understand that God is at once just and compassionate, merciful and true. They will know that they have been blessed and invited into a rich relationship with Christ. They will understand that they have been gifted and called as his "workmanship, created in Christ Jesus to do good works, which God prepared in advance for (them) to do" (Eph 2:10). They will know that they are accountable to God alone for their faith and the choices they make. We pray with all our hearts that they will choose to receive what God has to give, and that they will grow in Christ to become a blessing to the world.

Our kids need this. Our world needs this.

APPENDIX: WISDOM FOR SPECIFIC CHALLENGES

APPENDIX A

Self-motivated, Responsible Kids: Messes, Chores, Not Listening, Homework and Grades

I (Lynne) can remember standing in the middle of my messy living room one day, almost paralyzed. I knew I had in mind to actually get something done, but by the time I figured out what tasks the kids were deftly avoiding as they whizzed by, I had no brain power left to accomplish my own tasks. Trying to keep all of us on track at once resulted in nobody being on track. I felt like a sailboat in the middle of a lake and, as soon as I got a little wind in my sails, another little speedboat (a.k.a. Jackson child) would buzz by with a question or a need and I would bob in their wake with sails flapping. None of us was accomplishing much of anything in terms of responsibilities. To put it in a more positive light, the area of household responsibilities was quite a "growth area" for us over the years.

If the goal is to develop children who want to be responsible, not just children who are under the thumb of a watchful parent, it requires creative, proactive effort instead of just consequences. Such challenges benefit from an integrated approach that incorporates all the principles for effective, heart-connecting discipline.

Cleaning Up Messes

Practical/Biblical rationale: Cleaning up our messes decreases stress, honors those we live with, makes it easier to find things and helps us welcome others into our home.

I prepare my heart—What's going on in me? Asking these questions can help prepare your heart:

Am I taking personally the messes my children leave or feeling that I am being taken for granted? Am I worried that I am raising a future slob? Am I frustrated about a messy spouse or my own lack of cleanliness? How does any of this affect how I respond to my child? Sorting this out will help me to make more effective choices.

"You are loved"—How can I connect or empathize with my child?

We can happily join our kids in the cleaning or doing chores. After all the Bible tells us "Two are better than one, because they have a good return for their work" (Ecc 4:9). Empathise by letting them know that Mom and Dad understand feeling overwhelmed by a task, and share an example.

If we make cleanup fun and then gradually fade out our own help over time, children will be set up to better enjoy and value cleaning up. One day I (Lynne) was trying to figure out a different consequence for messes at our house. I dared to ask the Lord, "What would you do if they were your kids?" I was pretty sure his answer was, "I'd clean with them and enjoy the results." My immediate tongue-in-cheek response to God was, "Rats, you would, wouldn't you!" But this insight helped tremendously as I shifted my focus from dictator to joining and encouraging my children in their cleaning attempts.

"You are capable"—What might help my child be successful and/or avoid misbehavior?

Break the task down. Power struggles over cleaning often happen because a child is simply overwhelmed. Help a child break down the job into whatever size task he can manage. Designate a specific, manageable area (e.g., put a hula hoop or circle of rope around a section of mess) and tell him to come find you as soon as he gets that section done. Encourage and affirm (even dance a jig in the clean space), and offer a little help as needed to keep momentum up. Try to call it quits before he gets distracted or discouraged so that he finishes his work feeling successful. Even if it's a small success, it will build more success over time.

Eventually children can take responsibility to break the task down or figure out what else they need to do to be successful— i.e., music or snack while they work, visits from a parent at certain intervals, etc. Ask, "What do you need help with to be successful?" It will engage their problem-solving and increase their ownership of the task.

It's helpful to build cleaning into a routine. We do this by letting go of our efficiency goals and taking the time needed when kids are young to involve them in cleaning routines. Kari, the single mom who lived with us, would clean up the toy area with Eli every evening before they came upstairs to eat. It was second nature, no arguments, and because the mess didn't build up, it was not overwhelming. One evening, when Eli was two, Jim went down to tell them dinner was ready. Without another word Eli started putting toys away.

"You are responsible"—What consequence best teaches my child responsibility for his actions?

Do-over/Practice a right response: If a child drops something in a common area, you can have her practice putting it away several times, starting from whatever she was doing before she dropped it. This helps her learn a "neatness routine" and not depend on a parent's reminder. For example, "Put your jacket back on, walk through the front door again and put it on the hook this time. Tomorrow, if you forget, you can practice that two times."

Lose the privilege/item: When children misuse or don't clean up their own things, or things they are privileged to use, they lose the privilege of using them. If toys, take them away by calmly saying, "You didn't take responsibility to clean up your toys, so you have lost them." Set a time frame and clear expectation about what the child must do to get the toys back. For example, "You can get these toys back once you show that you can take care of your other toys by cleaning them up well for the next two days."

If the child complains, then validate their feelings by saying, "It's hard to lose your favorite things, isn't it? Can you tell me what you need to do to get the toys back?" The child will either repeat or keep complaining. If he repeats it, affirm his listening. If the complaining continues simply say, "I can see that it won't help to talk about this anymore now. That's okay, I know it's frustrating and you're pretty upset right now. If you want to ask later what is needed to get your toys back, let me know." Work hard to stay graceful and calm, and then walk away and don't engage that child again until he is respectful.

Other ideas: Helen is the mom of twins, and she valued a neat house. She would tour the house every night before the kids' bedtime and pick up any of their stuff left out and put it in a box to be ransomed the next day with a quarter from their allowance to pay for her effort. She was calm about it, and kindly matter-of-fact. The twins often scrambled just before bedtime to clean up, and over time made a habit of keeping things mostly picked up.

If a child just can't clean up after himself, then store most of the toys and work with small numbers of toys. Help that child learn to organize what he has left available to him. He can earn other toys back slowly by keeping the toy area clean.

In our house, Legos™ were everywhere. Noah loved them and Gramma loved giving them to him! They often carpeted the playroom and, like little landmines, gouged any unsuspecting barefoot adult. After struggling with this issue for a long time, I (Lynne) told Noah that he had the option to put them away for quite a while or organize them. He and I set aside some blocks of time and I guided him as he developed a system of categories, containers with little drawers, labels, etc. As we sorted, he realized that he had more than he needed, so he gave some away and sold some. He discovered that his new system helped him to find the pieces he wanted and make even cooler creations, so he was eager to maintain the system.

Chores and the Family Team

Biblical rationale: In a family, we all need each other. We are a team, and we share in the responsibility of the household. "God has arranged the parts in the body, every one of them, just as he wanted them to be" (1 Cor. 12:18). Each child has a special contribution to make to the body of Christ, and to whatever group she is in, including her family. When everyone contributes, everyone benefits. One child's service to the family is a blessing to other family members.

I prepare my heart—What's going on in me?

Consider these questions: Is my family's pace of life so intense that expecting and growing in routines for cleanliness and responsibility are unrealistic? Do I feel resentful and alone in taking care of the house because it's easier to do it myself than to get others to follow through? What could I do to make an adjustment and simplify either our activity level or my expectations of myself? Am I nagging more than I'm encouraging or affirming?

"You are loved"— How can I connect or empathize with my child?

How might I empathize with or validate children who have short attention spans and love to play, not work, while helping them learn to do the chores? How can I be sure to enjoy chore time with my kids? If my children complain about and avoid chores, an essential part of the solution is to nurture a culture of joyful teamwork in my family, which prepares them for faithful service in the body of Christ.

The importance of building joy and teamwork into chores was graphically illustrated by the contrast between our interactions with two different moms in one week. Michelle had been required to do chores when she was young and there were strong consequences if she refused or protested. She shared her discouragement about the impact of this with Lynne one day over coffee. She now generally dislikes housework and quickly feels resentful and critical if she thinks she might be doing more than her share.

A few days after that conversation, we joined our friend Jerilyn at her cabin and she welcomed us with joy. She refused to let us put our fresh sheets on the bed, and said, "Oh, no. You have no idea how fast Gracie and I are at this!!" Her 12-year-old daughter Gracie grinned— she knew the drill. The two of them whisked the old sheets off and got the new ones on in no time, laughing about their blinding speed and amazing skill. Jerilyn had been widowed with young children, but she nurtured joy in teamwork as a family, even to the extent of getting three used lawnmowers. Jerilyn, her son Paul, and Gracie all mow the cabin's large lawn at the same time. Their motto about family chores is, "If we all work together, we'll get it done in no time!" There is never a need for discipline or consequences for avoiding chores, the kids serve eagerly and diligently.

"You are capable"—What might help my child be successful and/or avoid misbehavior?

When children have choices and input into how chores are distributed, their engagement and cooperation increases immensely. One family had a Sunday-night meeting each week to eat a special meal, have fun together and brainstorm any challenges, including chores. Chuck told their story:

> We made a list of all the things that needed to be done to make sure that the family would run in a way that everyone got at least some of the things they thought were important. Laundry, dishes, and cleaning rooms were important for Mom and Dad. Play dates, eating, and free-time were the important kid issues. None of the kids were required to attend, but they did because they wanted a say in the rules, which would apply to everyone and last for one week. We'd reevaluate weekly until we found something that worked for everyone.
>
> At one particular meeting it was brought up that the kids were not putting dirty laundry where it needed to be when it was supposed to be there. We asked the family what ought to be done about this, and several of the kids had ideas. After hearing them all, the family agreed that for one week there would be a warning ten minutes before the laundry deadline. After that week whoever was late needed to fold the laundry for the rest of the family, which rapidly solved the problem. Involving the children this way kept us from the easy default of nagging and lecturing the kids, and it gave them a sense of pride of ownership in the family plans.

The great thing about these kinds of meetings is the way everyone has a voice and there is a strong need for compromise. And sometimes the kids think of their own effective consequences. (For downloadable information regarding family meetings, see our website at www.connectedfamilies.org under Parent Help—Free Stuff.)

Children need clear expectations. I had been frustrated by ten-year-old Noah's lack of thoroughness and what I considered his poor efforts in cleaning the bathroom. It dawned on me that I (Lynne) was expecting him to just know how to do it without ever actually breaking it down for him. So we started over and cleaned the bathroom together while I guided him in understanding and writing a step-by-step checklist of tasks that was then taped to the inside of the cupboard. He felt invested in the work instead of being ordered around, and he became a faithful bathroom cleaner.

Enlist ownership of results. When you've given a child a task, ask, "How will you know you've done a good job?" Invite the child to be as specific as possible in describing what a good job will look like. If the description does not meet your expectations, graciously clarify what you expect.

When he was 16, we paid Noah to do a variety of extra small jobs around the house. The workmanship was haphazard and our impulse was to criticize his effort by pointing out his deficiencies and pay him a reduced wage as a consequence. But we wanted him to be more thoughtful about the expectations he should have for himself so after discussing it between ourselves, Lynne said, "Looks like you've gotten most of today's list done. I want you to evaluate how it went. What do you think are the characteristics of a diligent worker? What would an employer be looking for in someone who does a really good job?"

He answered, "Someone who works efficiently, and doesn't get distracted," and then continued, "And does careful, high-quality work."

"Those are good ones," Lynne commented, and then added, "And probably doing thorough clean-up after a job is done. So, on a scale of 0 (the worst possible job) to 10 (the best possible job), how do you think you did?"

He rated himself about how I'd have rated him on each of the characteristics, averaging about a five. We gave him the "salary range" we were considering and told him we would pay him what he honestly thought he deserved based on the quality of his work. He actually chose an amount slightly below what we were thinking.

A few days later we gave him another list of jobs. On this one he recorded work times for each job much more accurately. He told us he worked pretty hard and got distracted only once to check emails. He rated his work a six or seven and asked for a wage $1 higher than for his first list. He definitely seemed to feel better about his "job performance" on this second try.

Connect well at transitions. When a child is engaged in a favorite, engaging activity, it is difficult to transition into chores. The more fun the activity and the tougher the chore, the more overwhelming this transition is. I can connect with a brief shoulder rub as I explain their chore or offer a quick snack before they get started. I can even ask, "It's time to get the dishes loaded now. What will help you get started?" I also can build some "cooperation momentum" by making a few very simple requests—on the level of, "Could you get me a tissue?" "Would you please toss this in the trash for me?" They are likely to comply with something so simple, and this gives me something to affirm. "Thanks, that was helpful," helps my child feel capable and helpful and gets the cooperation ball rolling.

"You are responsible"—What consequence best teaches my child responsibility for his actions?

Practice a right response: If kids don't follow through on a chore, a logical consequence is, "Now you have your first chore to do, but because you resisted or didn't complete the chore as expected, you'll have this other chore as an extra chance to practice responsibility." I can remind my kids that learning responsibility is an important part of walking in God's calling.

Lose the privilege: It's reasonable to withhold immediate general privileges if chores are not completed. "You may not go outside until your chores are done." Looking for loss-of-privilege consequences that are directly related to the chore is even more effective, i.e., "It seems your phone distracted you a lot from your chores today. We'll not keep paying for your text messaging if you don't contribute responsibly to household duties." Or, "Since you didn't do your part to clean the dishes, you'll be responsible to take care of your own meal and clean-up tomorrow night." Or, "Since you left your laundry all over the couch, I picked it up and you'll get it back when you demonstrate responsibility for your other chores."

Other Ideas: Chores come before privileges. Mason was ten and perfectly capable of feeding the dog, but he always managed to procrastinate with the chore. His mom, Rachel, either badgered him into doing it or he had so many emphatic excuses that it was easier for her to just feed the poor pooch. In a coaching session she made a plan to clearly affirm that they were a team to keep the household running smoothly, and they all had chores to do before dinner. Hers was fixing the meal, his was feeding the dog, and his sister's was emptying the trash. Each person could eat when their job was completed. Rachel light-heartedly quoted the verse, "'If a man will not work, he shall not eat'" (2 Thess. 3:10b). Mason adamantly begged and argued to do his after dinner, but Rachel calmly stood her ground and the problem was solved. Once he got into that routine, Mason actually felt good about being responsible.

Chore systems: Most parents employ various systems to help their children stay on track with chores. The most helpful one we've seen for preschool/elementary aged kids is the P.E.G.S. (Parental Encouragement and Guidance System) found at www.familytools.com. Parents can also order a jar of "Choose a Chore" or "Pick a Privilege" discs to be used as consequences or rewards.

Distractibility/Poor Listening and Following-through

The listening issue can sometimes be difficult to identify. It could be that kids hear what we say and choose not to do it. This is ignoring. Ignoring is more about defiance, which is covered in the Appendix section. Sometimes the kids hear what we say, intend to do it, but get distracted by something that is more fun. This is distractibility. Then, of course, sometimes kids have poor listening skills and truly do not hear and understand what is expected of them, even if we think they do. Many parents treat distractibility and poor listening as if it is defiance. This is not helpful at best, and hurtful at its worst, because kids who have a hard time listening and following through are not necessarily defiant kids. But to treat them as if they are tends to discourage them and form a belief in them about what bad, defiant people they are. Once they believe it, they act it out.

While it may be hard to figure out whether kids are ignoring, listening and forgetting, or truly not listening, the key to discerning is to treat the distractibility/listening issues first. If you work through the following ideas and the kids still do not follow through, then it is likely a defiance issue.

Practical/Biblical rationale: Careful listening honors the speaker and is a helpful skill for school, work, and family. "Everyone should be quick to listen, slow to speak and slow to become angry" (James 1:19).

I prepare my heart—What's going on in me?

Consider these questions: Am I modeling the listening I want from my children? What would my kids say about me as a listener? Do I make it hard for kids to really listen because I'm too stressed to communicate clearly and respectfully? Do I feel invalidated or like a failure as a parent when my kids ignore me?

As a home-schooling mom of teenagers, Sharon gave many instructions/requests to her children. She often felt frustrated and unfulfilled in this role. After going through one of our classes, she began to get in touch with some of her emotions under the surface of her interactions with her kids. Sharon recognized that one of the reasons it was hard to get them to listen and respond was that she didn't feel worth listening to. She realized that much of what she said was delivered with shame and that she lacked the confidence needed to enlist good listening. This started her on a journey of learning God's grace and his value of her that significantly improved her confidence and her relationship with her children.

"You are loved"—How can I connect or empathize with my child?

We often say, "Kids who feel listened to feel valued. Kids who feel talked at feel managed." If we want our kids to feel loved, we must learn to listen to them. If we want them to learn to listen, we must first listen to them. If I want a child to clean something up I can connect for a few seconds by listening. Like this: "Peter, you're really going at it. What are you working on?" This reminds me and my child that I'm dealing with a precious child here. Then I can smile, ask for some eye contact and give my clear instruction. Now the instruction will fall on much more "fertile soil" It's amazing what a difference this can make. It helps my child follow through and prepares me to deal with issues more kindly if he doesn't.

"You are capable"—What might help my child be successful and/or avoid misbehavior?

Getting kids to listen and follow through with a task requires a warm but clear instruction. Once I've given the instruction, asking my child to repeat it helps him get in the habit of good listening. Then I can affirm him for listening well and hold him accountable to follow through without delay.

Because it is natural for parents to give more attention to children when they don't listen than when they do, children can easily develop a self-perception/identity as a poor listener. One way to build my young child's skills and an identity as a good listener is to play listening games, i.e., play Simon Says, or hide a few objects in different places around the house and see if they can listen well to the clues to find them. The next time I'm giving a task request I can remind them of their success at listening during the games.

"You are responsible"—What consequence best teaches my child responsibility for his actions?

Practice a right response: When a child doesn't follow instructions, I can put her in a time-out spot and ask her to repeat the forgotten or disregarded instruction for one minute. When the time-out is over, she is free to go complete her task, which now should be ingrained in her mind. I can also give her a tablet and have her write down whatever task(s) she had been told to do. This puts the focus of the time-out on solving the problem and learning a strategy for being responsible rather than making the child just feel bad for what was done.

I can also use listening practice as a consequence for poor listening, i.e., "Now you are going to get an extra chance to practice listening carefully. Do five jumping jacks and then put the scissors away." Or, "Put all the clean forks into the silverware drawer, and then the spoons." Then, "Can you repeat what I asked?" When the child can repeat it, "Nice job listening!"

Lose the privilege: If there is a certain activity that often keeps a child from listening and following through, that activity can be a privilege that is lost, i.e., screen time, a specific toy that distracts them, a cell phone, etc.

Make restitution/reconcile: When kids don't listen, they dishonor the one who is speaking. I can explain that it takes extra time to follow up with a child who hasn't listened well and then ask the child to help me complete one of my tasks or chores to make it up to me.

Homework and Grades

Biblical rationale: Education is a privilege that deserves our passion and diligence. Good work habits with homework pave the way for future opportunities and practice the diligence children will need to "do (the) good works God prepared in advance for us to do" (Eph. 2:10).

I prepare my heart—What's going on in me?

Consider these questions: What shame might I have about my own school performance? To what extent am I getting my value from how well my child does in school? Do I have anxiety about my child's future academic success? Are any of these factors making me more intense and reactive about my child's homework?

"You are loved"—How can I connect or empathize with my child?

Consider Mitch and Andy's story from chapter 5. Is my attitude loving when dealing with homework issues? Is my child convinced that I truly love him no matter what his grades are? If not, what can I do to remedy that?

One fall there was a huge variation in the our children's report cards. Bethany and Noah's report cards had grades that might elicit a parent's "Ya make me proud, Kid," kind of response, but Daniel got rather "multi-faceted" grades. I (Lynne) was ready to have a firm talk with him about improving the low grades. This probably would have been about as frustrating and unproductive as most of my other "firm talks" a.k.a. lectures.

Jim wisely recognized the disparity in grades as a great opportunity to communicate to all three children that our love for them is unrelated to their success. We got the kids together and announced, "We are going to have a Report Card Party to celebrate the fact that we love each of you absolutely unrelated to your grades or success!" They were a little surprised, but delighted. We had a special dinner and then ran around the house like loonies, whooping and hollering and firing Nerf guns at each other. Popcorn and a game rounded out the evening. We all had a blast, but of course the child with the lowest grades seemed to have the most fun!

The next day we sat down with Daniel and asked him how he felt about his grades, starting with his strong subjects. When we got to the low grades he felt safe to express his discouragement and join us in making a plan to improve the grades. Daniel learned two important lessons from this experience. First, that he was responsible for his grades, not us. Second and far more important, he experienced a vivid illustration of unconditional love that he still occasionally references, more than a decade later.

"You are capable"—What might help my child be successful and/ or avoid misbehavior?

Oftentimes children are trying to do homework in a chaotic environment while a parent gets dinner or some other task is being done. The child, who may already feel anxious, is distracted by the chaos, making the task even more difficult. Any attention from the stressed parent too often happens when the child gets distracted or complains that he can't do it. These factors are bound to increase his discouragement and avoidance.

Parents can model and affirm good work habits by sitting across the table from the child in a quiet environment and doing their own "homework," such as reading, working on bills, etc. This modeling is a powerful calming and focusing influence, and you can give a quiet thumbs-up as you notice your child working hard.

Another significant issue is a child's energy level while trying to do homework. It helps to prep their body and their brain because after a long day at school, children are often exhausted and unfocused by homework time. Simple adjustments like doing vigorous physical activity before the homework, sitting on an exercise ball instead of a chair to provide constant gentle movement, or having a sport bottle to hydrate with and suck on can help significantly. Chewing gum or nibbling on a crunchy snack also helps keep kids alert and focused. Plan short movement breaks as needed to keep energy up, such as a jog around the house, jumping jacks, swinging. For more information about helping your child regulate his energy level, go to http://www. alertprogram.com.

"You are responsible"—What consequence best teaches my child responsibility for his actions?

We have seen many efforts to control grades backfire. Kids inherently know, "these are my grades. Why are my parents acting as if they are theirs?" So when parents put more energy into getting kids to keep up grades than kids do, the kids tend to either rebel further in order to keep a sense of control, or they comply without internalizing a sense that their grades are theirs. Learning to support kids to take responsibility for their abilities in this realm can be tricky, because this is one of the few areas of discipline where there are regular reports and updates about progress (report cards!). The ultimate goal is to have a child hold their report card in hand and say and believe, "I am fully responsible for these grades." Parents can play a significant role on the road to this goal. To do so requires skill in walking the tightrope between too much and not enough engagement. The following story illustrates this balance.

Brandon, the oldest child of a highly successful doctor, felt quite a bit of pressure from his parents, Brad and Rochelle, about homework and grades. They nagged him to get his homework done and punished him for low grades (mostly C's and D's) by eliminating his cell phone privileges. This infuriated him so he "punished" them by arguing and manipulating incessantly about it and getting even lower grades. In his mind, if he got good grades, they would "win." They were in a tailspin and came in for coaching.

The process started by helping Brad and Rochelle get to the place where they could let their son's grades be his responsibility and not theirs. As we began to discuss some of the reasons for Brandon's difficulty with focus and organization, his dad realized that he had had similar issues as a kid. His empathy definitely encouraged his son. We then focused on their strengths as a family: What was going well in their relationship? What did helpful encouragement from his parents look like? In what areas was Brandon working hard? How could his strengths in those areas help his homework challenges? We also worked together to develop strategies for organization and regulating his energy level while studying. Brandon agreed to check his grades online once a week and let his parents know if he needed help with anything. They decided together to pursue assessment and help for what might be ADHD issues.

Because Brandon felt understood and supported during this process, he was able to admit that he had been discouraged about his grades and truly did want to do better. I asked him what his goals were for his next report card and he said confidently, "B's." His mom immediately chimed in, "Don't you think you could get an A in music or art?" I reminded her that it was important for him to own his grades and, that if he achieved his goal, he just might feel encouraged to shoot a little higher. She agreed that B's were a good goal and the family implemented their plan. Brandon's next report card was his best ever, averaging right around a B.

So does this mean that parents totally give up expectations regarding homework and grades? Of course not. Hard work earns privileges. It is quite reasonable to have a family rule about responsibility before privileges such as "No screen time before chores or homework." If a child consistently struggles with getting glued to a screen while "forgetting" her homework, parents can simply reserve screen activities for the weekends. The medical journal *Pediatrics* (vol. 118 #4) reported that screen time has a detrimental effect on academics primarily if it occurs during the school week. So it can be a helpful, logical consequence to lose this privilege if a child is struggling in school.

Sometimes the problem with homework is getting it done; sometimes it is turning it in. Working with teachers can be critical to helping children learn to take responsibility. Another couple, Chuck and Karlene monitored but did not try to control their daughter Adrianne's school performance. They determined as much as possible to let their daughter "own the problem and experience the pain" from her actions. Adrianne was a delightful but scattered child who required daily reminders to take her backpack to school. One morning, after explaining to her that she was very capable of remembering her backpack and would no longer get reminders, they let her race down to the bus without it. Even though he knew it was the right strategy, Chuck had a knot in his stomach as he watched his daughter go.

The teacher called and was not supportive of this approach because missing assignments were a hassle and essentially made a student's irresponsibility the teacher's problem. She insinuated it was the parents' responsibility to make sure children came to school with their backpacks. Chuck empathized with the teacher but said, "How could we make this Adrianne's problem?" Together they agreed that when Adrianne forgot her backpack, she would be held in from recess to complete the assignments she had due that day. This was necessary only a couple of times and she began to bring her backpack regularly. Adrianne learned an important lesson: she was responsible for her schoolwork, not her parents or her teacher.

APPENDIX B

Peaceful Daily Routines: Mornings, Meals, Screen Time, Bedtime

I (Lynne) can remember many mornings where I spent some time reading and praying before the little darlings arose, gearing up for the day ahead with a bit of uneasiness. It was helpful refreshment, but I still often found the day unraveling before I even herded the kids to the breakfast table. Over the years I learned many helpful ways to move children through daily routines and tasks more easily and peacefully. The transitions to and from daily routines provide great opportunities to build habits that prepare my heart, connect with my kids and develop important values and skills.

Mornings/Getting Ready

Biblical rationale: How we start our mornings as a family often sets the tone for our day. Being aware of God's love, and our love for each other, in the morning helps us all to be encouraged and responsible as we get ready to face our day. "The LORD's lovingkindnesses indeed never cease, For His compassions never fail. They are new every morning; Great is Your faithfulness" (Lam. 3:22–23, NASB).

I prepare my heart—What's going on in me?

Consider these questions: What feelings and expectations do I have about mornings with my children? Do I feel responsible for every aspect of getting them ready to go? Do I begin each day by seeking God's mercies for me and my family? (see Lamentations 3:22-24)

Do I let my stress level set the tone for the day?–"C'mon, c'mon, we've gotta get going."

After attending a "Discipline that Connects" workshop, Joe asked what he could do to get his teenage daughter to wake up more quickly and to talk to him while he drove her to school. He was deeply disappointed and resentful that the connection he had hoped for in the mornings was lost in her crabbiness, silence, and an iPod. He had a hard time accepting that Allison just wasn't a morning person. So he was crabby too. He was needy for connection with a teen who simply was not very connective in the morning. Not a very good set-up for a loving, connected transition to the day. We suggested that he set a goal that was within his control. "Could you find a way to come to your daughter 'full,' and then look at this as a time to communicate true unconditional love—'I love you and enjoy being with you, even if you are silent and crabby?' This might be an important way to help Allison understand the love of her heavenly Father, who definitely loves her in that way." "Huh... Yeah, I could do that," he responded. Joe's expression changed from frustrated to encouraged as he looked at this situation with a very different perspective.

"You are loved"—How can I connect or empathize with my child?

Many families who have challenges with morning routine or leaving the house on time have benefited greatly from a little creative connection with their children before placing any "gotta get movin'!" demands on them. This can last from a few seconds to a few minutes and could be anything a child enjoys, such as snuggling time, a back rub, a short story or joke, or just a quick hug, etc. One dad said, "I learned that if I could get Anders laughing in the morning, everything went so much better."

Julian had a particularly difficult time helping his son Jack take responsibility to get out of bed and ready for school on time. The usual drill of alarm clock, nag, nag, nag, was leading to more power struggles and missed bus rides. Julian decided that he would become the alarm clock. Not sure if he would be a welcome presence, he made sure to stay light and pleasant as he quietly sang to wake his son. Once Jack began to stir Julian just waited for a bit and then asked, "how can I help you get up and get ready today?" Jack just groaned, but Julian was persistent. He began to rub Jack's shoulder, something he knew Jack liked. Soon Jack was awake enough and Julian lightly tickled him, which led to a pleasant skirmish. Julian made a quick game of getting Jack out of bed and then gave pleasant instructions about getting ready, which Jack promptly obeyed. Julian reported some months later that this connective approach had permanently changed the tone of their mornings.

"You are capable"—What might help my child be successful and/or avoid misbehavior?

Morning routines are definitely an issue in which children's bodies can work against them. Some children go from 0 to 60 before their parents can crawl out of bed, but other kids could lounge between the sheets until lunchtime. Scientists have discovered that there are true differences in people's brain function that affect how easily they get out of bed in the morning. Parents can help slow-moving kids wake up by providing a variety of energizing sensory experiences—i.e., lively music, a brisk back rub, gradually brighter light, etc. Jim used to wake Bethany up by rhythmically pressing on her back with both hands to push her down into the mattress. She loved the fun bouncing which helped to wake her up. A trick that many parents have reported works wonders is bringing the child a bottle of chilled sports drink or ice water before they get up. It works because of a combination of sensory, motor, and brain chemical reasons.

Once a child is out of bed, try to incorporate a quick, fun movement activity before she has to do her morning responsibilities. Eight-year-old Taria loved the challenge of finding one of her shoes in the morning. Her mom would hide it before she was up and then give her progressively more specific clues to find it. This got her moving and started the morning with an enjoyable game.

Many children also benefit from a simple list of pictures or words to remind them of their morning sequence. This can be kept in their bedroom or taped to the bathroom mirror. Or the night before, set out a line of their "supplies" across their bedroom floor, i.e., starting with all their clothing in the order they put it on and ending with a tube of toothpaste.

"You are responsible"—What consequence best teaches my child responsibility for his actions?

Avoid both reminders (nagging) and rescuing children (doing their work) because both these approaches communicate to kids that they are not responsible to get themselves out the door, and that you are. So what are some possible solutions to the pitfall of frequent reminders?

Establish clear-cut rules ahead of time about getting ready, and then stick to them. The family meeting format explained previously is really helpful for this. Here are some examples of rules families have developed:

- No breakfast until you're dressed and ready.
- Alarm clocks will be set earlier if kids aren't ready on time.
- Parents will stand behind any consequences for tardiness that the school gives.

- If kids aren't ready and parent must leave to be on time for her obligation, then, ready or not, children are put into the car as is.
- Last minute rides due to missed bus or poor planning cost the child $5.

The key to effectively enforcing any of these rules is for the parent to be peaceful and sympathetic, not angry or lecturing, toward the child, and then follow through with the rule when a child chooses not to get ready on time.

Lose the privilege: When our kids were little they were notoriously distractible dawdlers. So we requested they get ready a half hour or so ahead of leaving, before playing. We'd then check in a few minutes later. Any child not ready was sent to the time-out bench with clothes, away from the privilege of all those enjoyable distractions, until dressed. Any arguments resulted in further loss of privilege. We were consistent to follow through and they knew we meant business. The motivation to regain the privilege to get back and play improved their dressing speed drastically.

Another loss of privilege could be an earlier bedtime. If a child just can't get himself going in the morning, it is probably an indication that he is too tired, and can't handle the privilege of whatever is his current bedtime. A fifteen-minute earlier bedtime might help him either from the extra rest or the motivation to regain the later bedtime if he is consistently cooperative. Similarly, if a child doesn't respond to the warm greeting of a parent in the morning, he can lose that privileged way to wake up and learn to rely on a loud alarm clock.

The privilege of any game or item can be lost if it contributes to poor readiness. Whether toys, computer games, or other electronics, any time these draw a child's attention away from being ready in the expected way at the expected time, the losing of those privileges for a few days will help a child develop higher value of being ready on time.

Meals

We asked one wise mentor who had raised five outstanding, faith-filled children how he did it. "We shared our lives together around the table," he answered without hesitation. He went on to describe the richness of his family's commitment to family meals that focused on shared responsibilities, stories, prayers, laughter and tears. Unfortunately this experience is far from the reality for many families. We took an informal survey of young moms which revealed that meal-time won the contest for "Most Difficult Time of the Day." Everyone is cooped up together, movement is restricted, the mealtime noises are enough to aggravate anyone (my daughter still becomes irritated by the sound of a brother's noisy chewing), and smells and tastes are added to the sensory barrage. It's no wonder children often rock in their chairs, make loud noises, complain about food, antagonize a sibling, or simply climb down and try to escape. Stressed parents (who probably wish they could leave the table as well) often become demanding and controlling, and the volatile formula for mealtime mayhem is complete.

Biblical rationale: Mealtimes throughout Scripture are a celebration meant to strengthen family, faith, and community. Jesus shared joyous connection at meals with such a great variety of people that the Pharisees accused him of being a "glutton and a drunkard, and a friend of the worst sort of sinners" (see Luke 7:34). His early followers continued this important practice of connecting at meals. They broke bread (shared a meal) in their homes and ate together with glad and sincere hearts, praising God and enjoying the favor of all the people (see Acts 2:46–47).

So how can we bridge the gap between what God intended for meals and the everyday experience of many stressed families?

I prepare my heart—What's going on in me?

Consider these questions: How did my experiences at my family table growing up affect my expectations now? Was it stressful, peaceful? Was I forced to clean my plate and eat my brussel sprouts? What anxieties do I have about meals with my own family now? What expectations do I have about mealtime, and what do I do to set the tone for those expectations to be met? To what degree does my tone when communicating my mealtime expectations draw my kids to look forward to meal time? What do I do to represent the presence of Christ at our table?

"You are loved"—How can I connect or empathize with my children's needs?

Make a commitment and then discuss and establish with your family a value that meals are to be a relaxed time for eating and connection, not a feeding frenzy or TV time. Make a conscious effort to set a positive tone at the table. After a prayer of blessing and thanks over the food, parents can intercept the potential chaos or conflict by immediately structuring some positive connection.

- Share a simple scripture or "faith thought" of the day.
- Share affirmations of each other or highlights of the day. One family taught values and kept a positive focus by routinely asking either "When did you bless another person today?" or, "What are you thankful for today?" Another family desig-

nated one person each night to have a "special person place-mat," and family members took turns saying something they liked about that person, or something cool they noticed that he did that day.

- Utilize various online resources for fun "connection questions." Play the "Question Game" in which each person thinks up a question to ask another family member until all have asked and answered a question. This is also a great way to build social and listening skills.

- If children are struggling with sitting still or behaving appropriately, let them know that you understand how difficult it can be. Just this empathy may help them settle down. Don't use the mealtime to address and try to solve problems from other parts of the day.

"You are capable"—What might help my child be successful and/or avoid misbehavior?

Enlist your children's ownership and involvement in meal preparation. Children as young as three years old can help choose the food, prepare it, set the table and serve. As you work side by side and express appreciation for their helpfulness, your child is feeling good about himself before he ever gets to the table. Children can also have an important role in extending hospitality to others at mealtimes. An additional benefit: studies show that when children share in family responsibilities, they more strongly adopt their family's values.

Avoid power struggles over food. Parents are responsible for serving a variety of healthy food; children are responsible for what (and if) they choose to eat. Avoid all power struggles about what or how much your children eat. Power struggles over what kids eat ruin countless family meals, and research has shown that this is highly counterproductive in helping children learn to eat a healthy variety and amount of food. For practical tips regarding helping picky eaters expand their diet selection and settling squirmy kids at the table, see our website at http://www.connectedfamilies.org/help-for-parents/free-stuff/ for a download. One mom who used this download said, "I was amazed at how much more peaceful our meals were and how much better my daughters ate!"

Each family will have unique ways that kids misbehave at meals and unique ways to solve them. Help everyone contribute to a list of simple rules with a common goal of enjoying meals together. Find out what your children want mealtime to be like. Here are some possibilities for rules:

- **Eat what you want.** At each meal it is important to have at least one food that you know your children will eat. This helps you avoid both complaining and "cooking on demand" because your child dislikes all the food.
- **Honor the cook.** Complaining decreases dramatically when parents don't pressure children to eat their food. Children should learn that complaining about food dishonors the person who worked hard to make it. A more concrete variation of "Honor the cook" is, "You don't have to eat it, but don't complain about it." Be sure to model the honoring of the cook by thanking God and the cooks for the effort to prepare the meal.
- **Respect others at the table.** Have a child-friendly discussion about what it means to be respectful at mealtime and why it's important. Ask your kids what makes them feel respected at the table. Use these conversations to establish your family's rules for mealtime.

Once you decide on your rules, you can rehearse what they are and how they work. Parents can pretend to break the rules, children remind them of the rule, parents respond by correcting their "misbehavior" and demonstrating appropriate mealtime behavior. If desired, switch roles and have the children practice. This makes the rules clear and sets kids up for success in a light-hearted way.

"You are responsible"—What consequence best teaches my child responsibility for his actions?

Lose the privilege. If a child complains about the food, you can slide his plate out of reach for a break and gently say, "You can eat or not eat whatever you want, but to keep your plate you must be respectful." After a short time she can get her food back by respectfully asking. If a child repeatedly complains about food, invite her to work with you to plan and prepare a whole meal. Ask her to imagine how it would feel if several people complained about it.

Children can know ahead of time that if they are seriously disrespectful at the table, parents will calmly let them know they have lost their food privilege for the night. They may be hungry, but they will probably be wiser by the end of the evening.

If a child violates a specific "Respect others at the table" rule, she can take a break on a designated spot until she has a plan to be respectful. Another possibility is making restitution by completing the after-dinner chore for a person she has disrespected.

Suzanne's daughter, Katelyn, often had a difficult time in the mornings, including choosing what she wanted for breakfast. One Monday morning Katelyn refused the simple choices that Suzanne offered and began screaming at her, demanding that she cook pancakes. Suzanne's first impulse was to simply say, "When you yell like that, you won't get what you want," but she knew the transition from weekend to school day was hard for Katelyn and this could easily start her week with a huge meltdown. So she said, "If you ask me in a calmer voice, I will cook you pancakes. But you will need to cook breakfast for me one day later this week." Katelyn asked more respectfully, enjoyed her breakfast and had a good day at school. Later that week Katelyn insisted that her mom should choose a breakfast that would be a challenge to make. Katelyn really wanted to do a good job of serving her mom.

Screen Time

Nearly every parent has frustrations with their children's interaction with technology (electronic games, social media, TV, texting, etc.). There are two significant aspects to this issue—the nature/quality of the activities and their influence, and the quantity of time a child spends engaged with various screens. Some parents find themselves condemning the activities, "pulling the plug" and forbidding them, or policing their child's use and butting heads regularly about it. Other parents simply give up and give their youngster free rein.

Biblical rationale: Do a word search for technology in the Bible and you'll come up empty. But fortunately, the Bible does give wisdom in making decisions, particularly about pleasurable activities that could be addicting. Paul quotes the pleasure-seeking Corinthians who boasted, "Everything is permissible!" and deals wisely with them. They mistakenly interpreted their freedom in Christ to mean they could do whatever they pleased. That is not unlike dealing with a child glued to a screen who essentially communicates, "Don't interfere with my fun. I can do what I want."

In 1 Corinthians 6:12a we read, "Everything is permissible for

JIM & LYNNE JACKSON

me but not everything is beneficial." This verse addresses, "What's the quality of my activity, and is it truly beneficial for me?" What we dwell upon impacts us. Philippians 4:8 exhorts us to focus on things that are true, pure, and admirable. Years after we butted heads with Daniel about video games, he looked back on those days and reflected, "Single-player video games were a soul drain. When you guys would get me off the computer, it took awhile for real life to regain its relevance."

Paul continues his wisdom for the Corinthians, "Everything is permissible for me but I will not be mastered by anything" (1 Cor. 6:12b). This poses the question, "Am I really in control of my screen time or is it mastering me?" Don't expect a child to readily admit he's not in control of his screen time. On numerous occasions, however, we have seen kids feel much better about themselves after their parents have worked with them in positive ways to bring their screen use to a healthier level.

I prepare my heart—What's going on in me?

Technology and screen time is an important area to get in touch with my own anxieties. Am I feeling out of control because I don't know enough about the activity (TV show/game/site/text content)? Am I fearful that my child is getting addicted or engaged in harmful activities? Do have baggage of my own that I want to prevent my kids from experiencing as the power of technology puts more and easier access to dangerous choices at their fingertips?

Certainly there is a lot to be concerned about related to children's technology use. But if it's fear that drives my interaction, it will probably do more harm than good. Fear-driven parents often have critical, black-and-white judgments about technology which draw "fighting lines" in the sand right from the start. (The truth is that research has shown that moderate amounts, i.e., up to two hours a day, of non-violent/non-sexual screen time can be beneficial for social, academic, or coordination skills.) The older a child is, the more "relaxed curiosity" combined with a "come let us reason together" approach is helpful. To respond in this way, of course, requires that parents prepare their hearts.

Another important "what's going on in me" issue is, "What am I modeling to my child?" Am I admitting it if my own technology use is inappropriate or excessive? One kid insightfully said, "Dad, your BlackBerry is like my GameBoy. When are *you* going to get off of it?"

"You are loved"—How can I connect or empathize with my child?

It's a new world out there. For those of us who grew up with Pong, then PacMan, and then Missile Command, the new age of technology is overwhelming. In our overwhelmed state, we tend to take a judging posture. We say things like, "This can't be healthy. Where will this lead?" Or, "What has gone wrong with the way kids communicate?" Or, we just disengage from it all and leave our kids to their own devices. None of this connects us well with our kids.

On one hand, there is certainly great cause for concern in the way that modern technology has created a realm of influence on our kids that we never dreamed could happen. On the other hand, modern technology presents an opportunity that no other generation of parents has ever experienced with their children. If we want to address the concerns effectively and capitalize on the opportunity, we must learn to come alongside our kids with wisdom and grace, because unfathomably great is the power of technology to lure our kids into all kinds of experiences they simply are not prepared to handle. If we abandon them in it, they are almost sure to get hurt.

"Discipline that Connects" finds ways to use current technology as a way of staying in touch with our children—even encouraging them. Kids using technology are usually pretty easy to approach. Even defensive kids will let us near when they are nose deep in their screen. Take advantage of this and just be with the kids while they play and say, "I'm just going to hang with you for a while." Then, ask curious, safe questions to find out what a child really likes about his technology and how he thinks it's good for him. Have your child show you his favorite parts of it, and see if you could join in the activity with him. Work at observing and making a list of what's cool about it or what your child learns from it. This puts you in the role of a learner, not a critic, and lowers your child's defenses in a helpful way.

In the early days of texting and social networking sites I (Jim) was coaching a dad whose daughter was increasingly out of control with texting. "She sends at least a hundred texts a day," he said. The dad was irate about his rebellious teenage daughter's "addiction" to electronic communication. "And that's just the start of it. She spends at least two hours on "MySpace" every day, and "talks" to people she doesn't even know—or worse—to people who are faking an identity just to talk to her!"

As this dad inquired about how to deal with his daughter, he reported that he and she had "no lines of communication at all." I asked him what his conversations with her looked like. "That's the problem," he quickly claimed. "She doesn't know how to communicate the good old-fashioned way." Add a judging, condescending tone, and you'll get the picture of his mood. I empathized with him about how hard this can be, and then encouraged him to view this not as a problem to fix but as an opportunity to explore.

"So what would be the chance she'd communicate with you through text messaging?" I asked.

"I don't know how to text message," he responded.

"Do you know anyone who might teach you?" My tone implied an obvious answer.

"Really?" He asked. "Do you think she'd teach me?" His face lit up, as if discovering some powerful new idea.

"I don't know if she will or not. But you could ask."

Two weeks later I talked with dad again. He told this story:

> "It was so cool. My daughter taught me to text. We had fun together for the first time in a long time. Then we went to a school basketball game together. She ditched me ASAP. But I kept my eye on her and her pack of friends. I texted her, 'I luv u.' She didn't respond. I wondered if maybe this texting thing was just a flash in the pan. I tried again. 'Tx for teaching me 2 text.' Still there was no response. I was tempted to get angry, but I remembered that you said it would likely take persistence to truly connect with her. Then I got a surprise. When I went up to the concession stand my daughter sent her first text of the night, 'Where r u?' She'd been watching me—actually paying attention. I texted back, 'it's a secret.' We had fun playing a subtle game of hide and seek that allowed her to stay with her friends. The drive home was pleasant, and things have been much better ever since just because I took away my judgment and joined in her way of communicating. The coolest thing is that we actually talk voice to voice again too. I think I'm learning not to be so judgmental of everything she does, and she feels safer talking to me. Now I text her when I think of her. I just send simple things, not judging things or prying into her life."

There is no quick fix to troubled relationships, and the complex issue of the negative potentials of technology can still be addressed. But we can see how letting go of the "technology judgment" can create an opportunity to begin to reconnect.

"You are capable"—What might help my child be successful and/or avoid misbehavior?

We applied Ephesians 2:10 to our struggle with our son Daniel's TV use and gaming. "For we are God's workmanship, created in Christ Jesus to do good works [in His real-life, three-dimensional kingdom], which God prepared in advance for us to do." It was not an easy issue for us, but he knew we were honestly passionate that his potential to walk in God's calling would not be limited by excessive or unhealthy screen use. We were willing to make sacrifices to help him develop his real life gifts. Research shows that children who truly connect with the love of God and are involved in serving others, are at much lower risk for unhealthy behaviors. [1]

Children need persistent guidance and a positive focus on developing purposeful, alternative interests that are a fit for their unique gifting. It takes time and sensitivity to find out what it is that they love about their screen activities, and how we can help them give those desires expression in the three-dimensional world.

One presenter said it this way, "Unplug your computer games and just do real life with your kids! If they want to race cars, buy remote control cars or build some makeshift cars and go race for real! If they want to shoot stuff, get a bag of rubber bands or a some air-soft guns and go shoot stuff for real! If they want to play golf, or go bowling on a console game, then take them golfing or bowling for real! Do whatever you can to give them real life experiences in these things. Only then will they learn to conduct themselves in Real Life!"

We had many discussions with Daniel about how to balance his screen time with creative alternatives that were a fit for his unique bent. He gradually understood that screen time was "dessert for the brain," and he needed a real-world "healthy diet" to thrive in life. We paid the price both literally and figuratively, as we got him a camcorder, a digital camera, tree fort supplies, golf lessons, etc. These things provided three-dimensional, real-life fulfillment of the adventure, creativity, and conquest that he was seeking in his computer games. Each of those activities required parent involvement. I (Jim) worked on his tree fort with him and coached his golf team, but it was well worth it. He even used his digital camera to start a photography business that helped pay college tuition.

When children realize that we are on their side and want to help them become all they can be, they are much more likely to work with us instead of against us.

"You are responsible"—What consequence best teaches my child responsibility for his actions?

Because of the way the brain engages with screen, the transition from the one dimensional screen back into real life can be almost torturous. Kids typically ignore, ignore, ignore our elevating requests, and then either explode or fade quietly into withdrawal when they finally pull away. In neither case have we helped them learn about our expectation that they respectfully cooperate. It helps kids learn to take responsibility if they clearly know our expectations. So define your "exit strategy" ahead of time. For example, "I am going to give you a five-minute warning and set the timer. I will ask for eye contact from you and assurance that you understand. When the timer goes off I will come in to assure that you're done. If you are, great! If not, I will shut down the screen and you will have twenty minutes less tomorrow. Is this clear?" Ask your child to repeat the expectation.

Then, if the expectation is not followed, follow through. If the problem persists the next day it is fully reasonable to remove the privilege altogether the next day. Be sure to work at administering the consequence calmly and firmly, without forgetting to "prepare my heart," communicate, "you are loved," and "you are capable." You'll see these principles at work in the following story.

Jason was a typical third-grade kid who manipulated and intimidated his overwhelmed single mom, Lynette, into giving him way too much access to computers and TV. Most of his screen time ended with a habitual meltdown of protest at turning it off. Through some coaching Lynette started thinking about the challenge at a deeper level and make a new plan for constructive discipline. She told Jason that all this screen time was keeping him from developing the great potential that he had and that it was important to her to help him develop that potential. Lynette gave him some ownership in deciding what hours he could have screen time and what hours were off limits. For Jason to earn the privilege of each session of screen time he had to do two things:

1. Creatively use his time in between screen sessions (no whining about being bored). Together they developed ideas for creative or athletic activities and obtained the needed supplies.
2. Exit respectfully from the previous session. When it was almost time to get off the TV or video game, Jason's mom would give him a five-minute advance notice and then return at that time to calmly offer him the choice: "You can argue and stall and lose your next session or you can get off quickly and respectfully and keep your next screen time. Which would you like to do?"

It took a couple of sessions of testing, but Jason quickly learned that his mom was determined and would follow through if he argued and stalled. Of course, when he got off quickly, Lynette encouraged him with how helpful his wise choice was to both of them. Eventually he felt pretty good about all this and would brag to me about how well he was doing with his computer use.

Screen conflicts can get even more intense when there is inappropriate content involved and both parents and kids feel anxious, ashamed, and defensive about it. Sarah called me (Lynne). She was very worried about an impending conflict with her teenage son, Theo. Her husband, Tony, had discovered that a girl had been sending Theo pornographic "sexting" pictures of herself, and his texted reply clearly encouraged her seductive behavior. Sarah and Tony wanted to immediately and without explanation turn off the phone until they could deal thoughtfully with the problem, but they were concerned that it would set off another round of Theo's aggression toward his siblings, which had been a recurring problem when he was angry or discouraged. The strategy that I suggested was to avoid any statement that communicated, "We're angry at you, and we're going to stop that behavior," and work to communicate "We love you. It goes against our values provide you with a phone that's receiving harmful messages. We understand that's hard for you to lose your phone, but we're going to turn it off for now. We want to work with you toward some good long-term solutions." Though far from easy, this approach kept the parent's non-negotiables in place, without a volatile or controlling tone. Theo eventually felt respected and cared for rather than angrily controlled. Because the parents kept their anxious and angry responses under control, they were able to help Theo understand his own guilty feelings about what he'd done.

Bedtime

Bedtime can be a built in set-up for challenges because people are tired, parents and children alike, and tired people tend to abandon rational thinking and responding. Kids whine, parents are short and demanding, and they would often prefer to just stuff the kids in a box on the shelf until the next morning. For the kids their are many potential stressors. It's their last shot for attention, and perhaps they are anxious about being alone in their room. They can sense the urgency and frustration in parent's voices, and they sense in a parent's tone that mom is tired of them, which makes them more anxious for her to stay with them. Their out-of-sync nervous system makes it hard to shut off the noises, lights, and other sensations that keep them awake. Or maybe their schedule and daily rhythms are out of whack, and their bodies have trouble shifting gears to gradually calm down. Or maybe they have simply learned that by creating chaos at bedtime they get to stay up longer. If bedtime is a persistent challenge, and you've done everything you know how, understanding what's going on with you and your children is your most critical goal.

The three basic goals of bedtime management are to calm the child's body, calm his spirit and avoid "fertilizing" or rewarding any attention-getting or manipulative behaviors. If getting to sleep and staying asleep is a significant challenge for your child, an excellent, thorough resource is "Sleepless in America" by Mary Sheedy Kurcinka.

Biblical rationale: Psalm 127:2 says, "He grants sleep to those he loves." This implies that faith and trust in God allow us to sleep peacefully. Similarly, children sleep more easily when they feel secure and loved, and peaceful connection with a parent is an important book-end for their day.

I prepare my heart—What's going on in me?
Parents and kids alike tend to drag their stress and baggage from

the day into bedtime interactions. Helpful questions to consider are: Do I have chronic resentment at my kids for how tough they make bedtime? Or, am I feeling alone in this bedtime challenge and resentful of that? What specific leftover stress from my day might I be bringing into this interaction? How can I refresh myself with God's mercy for all of us before starting the challenge of bedtime?

"You are loved"—How can I connect or empathize with my child?

Children love it when adults understand how frustrating bedtime is for their active bodies and minds. When our kids were little we sometimes stomped off to bed, marching to a silly song we made up—"I hate bed, I hate bed! It makes me want to throw up. I wish that I could grow up. I hate bed...." It helped us all to release some tension before the kids hit the sack.

Some key messages can help set an encouraging "I'm for you, not against you in this" tone at bedtime:

- I absolutely love you no matter how you sleep.
- I can't stay with you at night, because husbands and wives need to sleep together. That's very important for strong families, and we really want our family to be strong. Single parents can explain, I can't stay with you at night because we sleep much more soundly in separate beds.
- Let's figure out what will help you be a successful, "grown-up sleeper." Then we can both get the rest that helps us feel good and have fun.
- I'm confident we can figure this out together.

It really helps keep connection (Love No Matter What!) alive at bedtime to ask, "At bedtime, what makes you really feel loved by

Mommy or Daddy?" This is obviously a great time to pray with children, but also to put a hand on them and proclaim a strong blessing of God's love and faithfulness on them. (See *The Blessing* by John Trent and Gary Smalley.)

If a child brings up irrational fears at bedtime, validate the emotion without substantiating the reality. "Oh, I remember when I was afraid of monsters. It seemed really scary at the time, but as I got older I learned there wasn't really anything to be afraid of. You'll learn that too over time." A silly name for the monster makes him seem less scary. If children insist on talking about it, make a date to chat about it the next day and be sure to keep the date.

"You are capable"—What might help my child be successful and/or avoid misbehavior?

Because of the importance of daily body rhythms, one of the most important things a child needs in order to sleep well is a consistent day-to-day schedule and a consistent bedtime routine. If a family's life is out of control, it is likely that the child will be out of control at bedtime also.

Sunshine in the morning and strong physical activity anytime up through late afternoon best sets up a child's biological clock to be ready for bed. Most kids need a predictable, gradually less active routine to calm their bodies after dinner. Many parents find that firm massage (or sometimes light stroking) is a great final activity to calm those little bodies. Parents can use the massage time to affirm anything they can remember that their child did wisely or well that day. This will calm their spirit and help them feel secure and enjoyed by us. It can also help a lot to provide children with something interesting to focus on, such as a lava lamp, fish tank, relaxing music, etc.

A general rule of thumb is to return for a visit before a child normally starts fussing, yelling or gets out of bed, even if this is initially a fairly short interval of a few minutes. Compliment your child for the nice job staying in bed quietly. Once she feels successful and secure that she is not abandoned, the intervals between check-ins can gradually lengthen. If a child gets out of bed, a relaxed, gentle statement like, "I can help you get back into bed," will avoid a power struggle and create much less anxiety than, "Get back to bed!"

For Ellie and her family, bedtime was the worst time of the day. Ellie was prone to anxiety and hated to be separated from her mom, Sonja, even at age 7. Sonja did her best to stay relaxed and affectionate at bedtime and keep a consistent routine. But when it came time for Sonja to leave each night, no matter what her mom tried Ellie still got hysterical, came up with elaborate, irrational reasons why she needed her mom to sleep with her, and frequently jumped out of bed screaming as Sonja left. This conflict put the family in an uproar because of course no one else could sleep. The battle would rage off and on for an hour or two, with both mom and dad in and out of her room in exasperation, until Ellie was exhausted and finally crashed. Act 2 of this melodrama was that she often woke up several times at night, yelling and demanding to either crawl into bed with her parents or have her mom stay with her until she fell back asleep. A psychologist had been working with her about this issue for months and had given Ellie a list of seven calming techniques she should use to fall asleep—to no avail. Various points-rewards systems had not worked either. I (Lynne) even suggested a specific behavior modification approach that didn't help for more than a few nights.

It dawned on me that we were all working hard to control Ellie's behavior, and doing very little to empower Ellie to control her own behavior. Sonja was ready for any new ideas, so I talked with Ellie and encouraged her to figure out how "brave" her body was feeling each night, and how long she could wait in bed quietly and peacefully before she needed her mom to come back for a visit. I said, "Even if it's just one minute, you figure out how brave you can be each night." "Oh, I think I can do 5 minutes," she said and smiled at her mom. "It's o.k. if it's 5 minutes, 1 minute or 10 minutes. It's most important for you to feel good about being brave."

Ellie gradually became more and more confident and peaceful at bedtime. When her mom said good-night, Ellie would let Sonja know when she needed her to come back for a visit. Her mom would return as requested for a few minutes to connect and rub her back, and then she would ask Ellie how long she could be brave until she visited next time. Ellie began to fall asleep within 10-20 minutes instead of an hour or two. Encouragement for Ellie's bravery replaced the previous frustration and consequences for her screaming and demanding. Because she was going to bed peacefully, she was sleeping more soundly. When I saw them again two weeks later they were both smiling and well-rested. One time Ellie even woke up at night, thought about going in to her parents' room, and decided to go back to bed herself. That was a huge success for her and she glowed with pride as she talked about it.

With older children who struggle with bedtime, parents can problem-solve bedtime conflict together. Discuss the natural consequences of the conflict on everyone involved and brainstorm what the family can do to have peaceful, connected bedtimes, including establishing rewards or penalties the kids develop.

Bedtime was a regular problem in our household. By typical bedtime the kids were wired but Lynne was fried, especially when Jim worked late. It led to chronic conflict until we all agreed that we didn't like ending the evening angry at each other and we wanted to do something about it. We started by talking about the frustrations we wanted to solve with some brainstorming. Together we developed a system of rewards for getting into bed on time and consequences for lateness or arguing. Every minute late translated into three minutes earlier bedtime the next night, and a week with five out of six respectful on-time nights earned each person a later bedtime with popcorn and a video on the seventh night—usually Friday. It wasn't a flawless system, and there were still rough nights sometimes, but it was definitely better. Our collaboration helped everyone to own the problem and build creativity and conflict-resolution skills. One of the plans that had the added benefit of encouraging reading, was that if the kids got ready early, they could stay up a little past bedtime reading in their bed. We got them each bed lamps, and this motivated them to often get in bed early to do some reading that actually allowed them to stay up a bit later. They truly grew in a sense of capability about preparing for their own bedtimes, and as young adults they now each have a value of decent bedtime and sleep time.

"You are responsible"—What consequence best teaches my child responsibility for his actions?

Practice a right response: It can actually be helpful for a child to practice his bedtime routine in the middle of the day, when no one is tired or crabby. For example, "Because you had a pretty hard time last night, today before you get your next privilege, you'll need to practice going to bed appropriately." When they practice this appropriately, affirm them for their success and talk about the natural consequences of cooperating when going to bed. Then you can remind them of the success they had during this "dress rehearsal" when it's time for the real evening "performance."

Make restitution/reconcile: Children who exhaust their parents with long drawn-out bedtimes can make restitution by lightening their parents' load the next day by doing some extra chores. We told our kids that if they challenged us about bedtime and drew our energy away from final cleaning for the day, we would leave the kitchen mess (or other mess) for them to clean the next day. Of course if they challenged us we did our best to follow through.

Lose the privilege: Whatever a child's current bedtime is, it's a privilege compared to the earlier bedtime he might have. When a child is uncooperative at bedtime, it may be an indication that she is too tired and needs to start earlier each night. Consistent cooperation at bedtime probably means she's getting enough sleep. So if a child continually challenges you about bedtime, an earlier bedtime may well be called for.

APPENDIX C

A Family Culture of Respect and Reconciliation: Whining and Meltdowns (for any age), Defiance, Lying, Aggression and Disrespect

Your boss, or spouse, or parent, or friend tells you what to do. For whatever reason, you don't want to do what they've requested. So you think of reasons why the request is unreasonable. You may even feel a temptation to do the opposite of what was requested. You may feel compelled to argue. Or you may think of schemes to avoid doing what has been requested. You may even consider doing your own thing instead—"just to show 'em!"

In a small way, this is the battle the apostle Paul talked about in Romans 7:21. "So I find this law at work: Although I want to do good, evil is right there with me." At the core of this teaching is selfish and inconsiderate desire. It's simply sin, a problem we all have—including our kids.

While typical approaches to treating misbehavior are intended to make the misbehavior go away, the "Discipline that Connects" approach is intended to help our children understand and take responsibility for their own sin and selfishness. This requires the difficult task of letting go of our need to immediately control our child's response and taking the stance of a graceful teacher and guide for our children as we address the underlying sin and selfishness (both ours and theirs).

Whining and Tantrums (for any age)

On the day a child is born, he cries and fusses to make his needs known. It's all he knows how to do. He gets rewarded as parents and others work hard to figure out how to meet the needs that prompt the crying or fussing. So kids learn that if they cry long enough and hard enough they'll get what they want.[1]

As kids grow into toddler years, it becomes the parent's job to help the kids unlearn their infantile behavior and replace it with more mature skills. Unfortunately however, many parents fail to do this job, and many kids grow up with well-honed whining and tantrumming skills.

In learning how to stay calm and respond wisely to tantrums, it's helpful to know that they are actually quite predictable in how they unfold. Research shows that there are three typical phases:[1]

1. Screaming and yelling
2. Physical actions - Kicking, hitting, throwing or banging things, or for older children, storming off and slamming doors.
3. Crying and whining - This is often when a child flops down onto the floor and sobs, or a teen collapses onto her bed in anger and frustration.

Simply knowing this sequence helps a parent see the whole process evolve. We can even comfort ourselves with a little internal humor as we silently observe, "Ah, Phase Two, coming up!"

Parents sometimes over-react to tantrums as if they were some major character defect in their young child. A different way to look at these outbursts could be that your child has limited understanding of his intense emotions, and even less ability to self-regulate those emotions. This is not to deny the selfish source of these outbursts, just to recognize a child's need for grace and growth instead of condemnation and control.

Biblical rationale: Everybody from Dr. Spock to Grandma has a different idea for how to deal with a tantrumming child. We've heard everything from spank him, step over her and keep walking, plop him in his crib, put Tabasco on her tongue, and more. There is no single answer for this aggravating problem, partly because the causes can vary widely. In the midst of all the possible responses, it's helpful to look for some guiding principles in how God responds to one of his own angry children. Consider his response to an outburst by the psalmist in Psalm 73:21–24:

> "When my heart was grieved and my spirit embittered,
> I was senseless and ignorant; I was a brute beast before you.
> Yet I am always with you; you hold me by my right hand.
> You guide me with your counsel, and afterward you will take
>   me into glory."

We can observe several important principles in this section. It appears that:

- God was not fazed by the outburst, nor condemning or controlling of it.
- He did not give into the psalmist's demands.
- God was present, loving and guiding the psalmist through his difficult emotions.

When we respond in this way we help our children understand the depths of our love and God's love for them in their worst moments. In the verses immediately following this section, the psalmist makes a passionate statement of his love for God, Psalm 73:25–26.

It's tempting to just focus on how to stop a child's annoying whining or tantrumming. But God has a more important, over-arching desire for his children: to learn to thoughtfully and respectfully ask for what's truly important to us and have a peaceful response to the answer. Philippians 4:6–7 says, "Do not be anxious about anything, but in everything, by prayer and petition, with thanksgiving, present your requests to God. And the peace of God, which transcends all understanding, will guard your hearts and your minds in Christ Jesus." Contentment regardless of the answer to the request is exemplified by Paul in Philippians 4:12, "I have learned the secret of being content in any and every situation, whether well fed or hungry, whether living in plenty or in want."

I prepare my heart—What's going on in me?

Consider these questions: Do I know how my child's whining or outburst makes me feel and how those feelings contribute to my response? i.e., do I become anxious or tense if my child is upset with me? How can I put her need for firm boundaries ahead of my desire for her approval?

Am I attentive to my child's first attempts to get my attention so I can guide him into a respectful request, or do I wait until he whines or escalates to a tantrum? Do I do an adult form of whining to get my child to quit whining? Do I match her meltdown with my own?

Two-year-old Garrett asked in a fairly normal voice, "Wanna get down," but his mom, Corrie, was deeply engaged in a conversation at dinner. He tried again, progressively louder and with more of a whine in his voice, until he finally started pounding the table and yelling, even smacking her once on the arm with his pounding. She turned to face him for the first time, glared at him and angrily said, "That is *not* how you get my attention!" Well, actually, it was exactly what he had to do to get her attention, and he got lots of it. In truth, Corrie's response was a reward, not a chastisement for his behavior.

Let's face it, whining and demanding children can wear parents out. If I don't have a strong and purposeful determination to *not* reward these behaviors, I can easily end up teaching my kids that it's a great way to get what they want.

Instead of focusing on stopping the whining, I can "prepare my heart" for this challenge by developing a clear vision to teach my child respect and self-control for his benefit, not my relief.

Some friends of ours used humor to keep themselves calm and light-hearted when their child whined. They explained to their kids ahead of time that they were going to play a little game to help them learn not to whine but to ask for things in a better way. The next time their daughter began to whine, Linda turned to her husband and said sweetly, "Mike, can you hear what she's saying? Her lips are moving, but I don't hear anything. She must be whining." Mike joined in the fun. "You're probably right; I don't hear anything either. I wonder what she's saying?" Ali caught on quickly and made her request in a regular voice, which received attention and encouragement from her parents. Even though their daughter was fairly intense and strong-willed, whining was not much of a problem in their home. The secret to the effectiveness was that the tone of the interaction was completely playful and not condescending or invalidating. When they could see that their children were truly upset, they wisely chose empathy instead of playfulness.

Research about tantrums shows that almost any intense engagement by a parent escalates or prolongs a child's outburst. This includes questions, commands, or any attempt to gain control, because it over-loads an already stressed child. What has shown to be most helpful is to either peacefully not respond while the child has a chance to self-calm, or use simple sentences to express what the child might be feeling and wanting. Sometimes a combination of both are helpful, according to the country's most widely read pediatrician, Dr. Harvey Karp. Either response requires that a parent be peaceful before engaging with an out-of-control child.[2]

"You are loved"—How can I connect or empathize with my child?

Whining and tantrums or meltdowns tend to escalate when a child feels his parent is against him. Simply communicating love when children are agitated and whining can help calm the child. Parents can use these times to communicate an important message: "When you whine (or demand), you won't get what you're whining for, but you will get my love—just as much as ever."

Empathizing with a whining or crying child is a powerful way to express love, without giving into demands. I can gradually help my child learn to communicate respectfully when she's upset by empathizing and "putting words in her mouth" as I restate more appropriately what she seems to be feeling and wanting. "You're really mad that you can't have this cookie right now. I love cookies too." It validates her and encourages self-awareness and communication without giving in to her demands. We have seen repeatedly that, from toddlers to teens, when a child feels truly understood and validated in what she wants, she is much more likely to calm down, ask respectfully and, if necessary, accept "no" or "later" for an answer.

Here's an example of how the empathizing approach might look like when your child is demanding you buy them some new treasure:

"I can see why you really want those Legos (or new jeans); they're really cool. I like that they are _____ (some details about this oh-so-desirable item)." This is very connective language that deflates a child's negative energy and prepares her for some instruction. "I can't give them to you when you ask that way, so we'll talk about a plan to get them when we get home."

"You are capable"—What might help my child be successful and/or avoid misbehavior?

Kids don't usually whine, demand or tantrum immediately when they want or need something. It usually begins with an indirect request like, "I'm thirsty." It's the kind of thing that either doesn't get much attention at all or that parents quickly act to remedy. The problem is, the child has taken no responsibility to make a request.

If I want to help a child learn at that first request to take better responsibility for what he wants, I can respond by saying, "You're thirsty, are you? How could you ask about that respectfully?" Usually the child already knows. If not, you can provide coaching.

We can usually predict some of the times when kids will start to whine. Anticipating these times and setting kids up to succeed rather than waiting for them to fail can be a very effective way to teach. Maybe it's at the mall when they pass that certain store and want candy or clothing. Maybe it's after dinner when they want to leave the table or to get a ride to a friend's house. If you know when kids might be most prone to start whining, you can set them up to succeed by saying, "So, it's about that time when I know you'll want to leave. How do you want to ask about that?" Kids will almost always ask appropriately given this opportunity. And when they do, you can affirm it and, if possible, grant their request.

Offering choices is another effective way to encourage a child. Presenting two acceptable alternatives to what the child is demanding often de-escalates the conflict and helps the child learn to look for options when frustrated. Two-year-old Eli wanted to be carried. "Carry me," he whined. Kari responded, "Eli, you know Mommy won't give you what you want when you whine. You can try again without whining."

"Noooo!" Eli lamented, testing her patience. "Carry me!" He stomped.

"Eli," she firmly but gracefully responded, "I guess you don't want to be carried badly enough to ask nicely. So I won't carry you this time." She turned and began walking toward her car. She offered, "Do you want to hold my hand or go all by yourself?" Eli whimpered, grabbed her hand and did not whine to be carried again for a long time.

Sometimes children who easily escalate to a tantrum do so because it pays off for them. They either get what they want or they get a lot of attention from their parents' big emotional reaction. Simply ignoring these children's meltdowns might be the most effective way to help them learn that they are capable to calm down on their own. (Parents can help them problem-solve or practice a better response later.) Some tantrum-prone children, however, truly feel anxious and out of control. They validly need to feel loved, understood and have some healthy control. These anxious kids may escalate quickly if a parent ignores them by walking off, because that leaves them alone in their distress which can be frightening for them. Helping these kids grow in capability requires a different approach.

Julie was overwhelmed by her intense, anxious three-year-old's tantrums. Abbie could tantrum for two hours straight about almost anything. Her parents were exhausted and felt as though they were walking on eggshells. Julie was elated one coaching session after we had been working on this. "I knew it could be a long tantrum based on how she started. I stayed calm, and I kept repeating in simple phrases how I thought Abbie was feeling—'You're mad right now. You didn't want to come home!' Abbie calmed down in only 45 minutes. I was so proud of us!" This was the start of a long process of Julie learning to stay calm and helping Abbie learn to express what she was upset about. Over time the tantrums grew shorter and shorter as Abbie developed skills for managing her intense feelings. Several years later, Julie looked back at their struggle. "Abbie is still intense, but also manageable, loving, smart, and very perceptive."

"You are responsible"—What consequence best teaches my child responsibility for his actions?

When children whine or demand they are motivated to get what they want, and this creates a tremendous opportunity for learning. You can invite responsible asking by peacefully saying, "I will consider your request when you ask without whining."

Whining and harsh demands were fairly infrequent in our house because the children knew that was a quick way to get neither attention nor what they wanted. With a no-expression and no-eye-contact response from Mom or Dad, they would hear, "I know you're frustrated, but how you asked for that wasn't helpful. Go set the timer for five minutes, and when it rings you can have a chance to practice asking nicely a couple of times." This wait-and-practice approach teaches helpful skills of quiet waiting and respectful asking. It also makes sure that a parent's anger and attention don't "reward" the whining. Once your child asks respectfully, you can celebrate with a reward of expressive affirmation, so that the child feels good about their success. These good feelings become motivators for future success.

Teenage "Whining"

Whining is not just a toddler trait. Fourteen-year-old Brooke loves to go to the mall with her mom and she has learned that if she begs and manipulates, she can get her mom to buy her some trendy clothing item almost every time they go. But her mom, Jennifer, decided that she was going to work at overcoming her need to be liked by Brooke. She knew (because she was warned) that the first time she tried some new ideas might be the hardest.

So Jennifer planned a trip to the mall and Brooke was eager to accompany. Jennifer let Brooke know that she wouldn't be buying her anything this trip. Brooke agreed with no argument. Jennifer was a bit surprised, but this is actually quite normal because the teen doesn't really believe it and will save the arguing for the real battle once she decides what she wants.

Sure enough, as they passed one of Brooke's favorite stores she started in. "Mom, I know you said you wouldn't get me anything, but there are some really cool scarves on sale here. They're pretty cheap. Can I get just a couple?"

"Brooke," Jennifer answered, "I was clear with you before we came that I'd not be getting you anything today. If you'd like to get the scarves with your own money, I have no problem with that."

"But Mom," Brooke's intensity rose, "it's buy one, get one free. We'd be stupid to pass it up, and it ends tomorrow. It'll be less than fifteen bucks and I can pay you back."

Normally this was when Jennifer would begin to waver. But this time she was prepared. "Brooke, I know I often give in to you about this kind of thing, but I realize this is not helping you learn to be more responsible. So my answer is not going to change."

"Seriously?" Brooke launched in. "You say you want to be with me for some shopping but then won't even spend fifteen bucks that I say I'm gonna pay back. What's up with that?" Brooke was on a mission.

So was Jennifer.

"Brooke, I really do want to spend time with you." Jennifer remained calm and matter-of-fact. "But if this is how you are going to act when we go to the mall together, we will have to find other things to do that won't tempt you to act this way. So if this continues, I'll not be bringing you to the mall again for quite a while. I'm not going to give this any more energy right now."

Brooke continued to rant and rave. Jennifer turned and walked toward the car, fighting every urge inside her to find some way to work this out. Brooke realized she was not going to get her mom to cave in this time and started following at a distance. They got in the car and drove silently home.

The next time Jennifer went to the mall she reminded Brooke that she had lost the privilege of going to the mall with her. She invited Brooke to think about a plan for how the demanding would not happen again and told her that when Brooke presented that plan, they would negotiate the right time for Brooke to accompany her mom to the mall again.

Jennifer learned a lesson about standing her ground, and Brooke learned that mom was no longer a pushover. Brooke continued to test Jennifer in other ways, but over time Jennifer applied the same principles to Brooke's demands and slowly Brooke became more responsible for her own life.

When children tantrum or are harshly demanding they also cause hurt in relationships. To help them be responsible for their actions, parents can encourage them to seek forgiveness. Like this:

"Honey, your yelling at me hurt my feelings a little, so before I carry you again (or bring you to the mall again), I want you to know that I forgive you for how you treated me, but you will have to apologize before I will do it again. If you feel sincerely sorry you can ask now. Otherwise you can wait. Let me know when you're ready."

This statement makes the children responsible for asking forgiveness, but lets them decide when they feel truly sorry. This can be tricky because we never know for sure if kids are authentically repentant. But if we force them to apologize right away, all they learn is that they have to say they are sorry when someone else decides that's how they should feel.

Particularly as children get a little older and are able to remember and process what happened, they can be held accountable to make restitution for the impact of their meltdowns. This can be as simple as stating, "Yelling and screaming adds stress to the family. Before you enjoy any special privileges, you can do something that adds encouragement and joy instead." Planning a family game, helping to make a special meal, etc., helps a child get out of the rut of misbehaving to feel significant or powerful, and can truly lift the tone in the family after the meltdown.

Defiance

We see it happen with kids of all ages. We say do this; they refuse. We say stop; they do it anyway. We say come; they dash the other direction. This is the classic my-will-against-your-will parent/child struggle. At the extreme, these kids get labeled as "Oppositional Defiance Disorder." (ODD). We learned some very important lessons about what these children need over years of working with kids who fit the ODD label.

The first mistake we see parents make when children are defiant is to get drawn into the power struggle by having their primary goal be to gain immediate control. The parent says, "Do this!" The child says, "No!" The parent feels challenged and makes the demand more strongly and the child responds with greater resistance and a battle ensues. Because the child's defiance triggers our reaction, we parents typically follow through with our fight, feeling justified in our anger and our actions in the name of dealing with disobedience. When this happens the kids either give in by complying (which is not obedience) and feel defeated, or they feel compelled to win by rebelling more.

When kids defy us by doing the opposite of what we ask, in a certain respect they hold up a mirror for us that shows whether we are walking according to the fruit of the Spirit, particularly peace, patience, gentleness and self control, or the deeds of the flesh, particularly hatred, discord, outbursts of anger, or selfish ambitions (see Galatians 5:19–22). The choice we habitually make will be as strong a teacher as any other choice we may make, especially if we have intense children who challenge us often.

If we are serious about bringing children up in the training and instruction of the Lord, the way we handle our child's defiance may be the most critical piece of parenting we do. We have worked with many parents who have most of the parenting journey down fairly well but who struggle to treat defiance with the fruit of the Spirit. These parents often see their kids rebel and make short- and long-term choices to stray away from God.

So we invite parents to set a new primary goal when a child is defiant. Make obedience a secondary goal and make accessing the Spirit and walking in the fruit of the Spirit the primary goal. We have repeatedly seen this approach gently guide kids toward sincere (as opposed to intimidated) obedience.

One possible response, when your child looks at you and says "No!" to your request, is to look back at the child and, in a relaxed, inquisitive tone, ask, "No? What's that about?" If the child can't or won't answer, then say, "I'm going to ask again in just a minute, and I expect you to obey what I ask. Is there anything I can do to help you succeed?" This will let the child know that you still mean business but that you are "for" him and not "against" him. It will also give you a chance to think of a wise, purposeful consequence if he chooses not to obey you. Then, with both of you in a better frame of mind, see what happens.

Since defiance is often related to one of the other topics covered in the Appendix, such as chores, messes, screen time, etc., refer to those sections for more specific ideas.

Lying

Most parents make it their goal to get kids to stop lying. It seems, at face value, like a reasonable goal, but it tends to pit parents and children against each other from the start because kids are bound to lie as they grow up and parents are bound to catch them. Over time, this can become a contentious hide-and-seek match in which the children get better and better at hiding their lies, while suspecting parents grow less trusting of their kids and work harder to catch them and punish them for their lies. We have seen this dynamic snowball until kids and parents utterly despise each other. This is why we advocate a different goal for parents relative to lying. We have seen much better success when parents seek to validate and place high value on truth-telling rather than putting big energy into punishing lying. This is not to say we don't confront lies, but we de-emphasize the punitive approach.

The goal of promoting truth-telling is validated by a research study conducted by Dr. Nancy Darling of Penn State University in which elementary-aged children were set up with the opportunity to tell a lie. She found that reading the "Never Cry Wolf" story to kids first (which emphasized the dangers of lying) did nothing to curb their lying during the experiment; most of them lied when given the chance. Reading a story which promoted the benefits and good feelings involved with truth-telling (based on the George Washington and the cherry tree story), reduced lying by 43 percent. Most of these children told the truth when given the chance.[3] The authors of this article also found that kids who are frequently punished for lying don't lie less; they just get sneakier and better at it.

So we are going to share an approach that places a high value on truth telling and treats lying with grace. We have seen this approach powerfully open children's hearts to the Holy Spirit's conviction about lying and telling the truth.

Biblical rationale: Jesus described his very nature as truth. "I am the way and the truth and the life" (John 14:6). True intimacy with people and with God depends on honesty. Telling the truth, especially if it is difficult for the other person to hear, builds trust—"Wounds from a friend can be trusted, but an enemy multiplies kisses" (Proverbs 27:6). False statements that sound good or smooth over a situation are the "kisses of an enemy." Habitual lying leads to hardness of heart and broken relationships. Knowing all this to be true, the paradox of teaching kids to tell the truth is to demonstrate grace when they lie, while advocating strongly for the benefits of truth-telling.

I prepare my heart—What's going on in me?

Research suggests that a primary reason kids learn to lie is that their parents model lying. Are you aware of any little ways (or big ways) that you are dishonest, and say what you think people want to hear? Beth was angry and punitive when her son stayed late at a party and then lied to her about the lack of parent chaperons. She failed to consider that before he left she had suggested a deceitful excuse to leave the party if there were no parents, "Just tell your friends you have a headache." The message was: lie to your friends to do what I want you to, but you'd better not lie to me.

What do you feel when your child lies, and how do your feelings affect how you respond? If your own hurt or anger is the primary driver of your response, then your child will feel guilty not because God says lying is wrong but because it upset Mom or Dad. So the child will either get craftier about not getting caught or take the lying elsewhere. Preparing my heart regarding a child who lies means that I learn to respond to my child out of my compassion and not my hurt.

You are loved—How can I connect or empathize?

The day I (Jim) stole polished rocks and lied about it, I learned about unconditional love. I was eight years old and loved those little polished rocks from the beaches of local lakes. So when no one was looking I took a small box of them, stashed it in my pocket, and headed out the door and down the sidewalk toward the car. Grandpa had been waiting on a bench on the sidewalk near the car, and quickly noticed my bulging pocket and strange walk (to cover the sound of rattling rocks). "What's that in your pocket Jimmy?"

"Nothing." I lied stupidly, as my package had already been discovered.

"Let's see what's in there." He remained gentle, but was visibly upset. I started shaking with guilt and fear. When I took out the rocks and handed them to him he didn't say a word. He clenched his jaw, turned, and started walking toward the store. After a few slow steps he turned back and motioned for me to come. I quickly obeyed. When we got to the entrance he handed me the box of rocks and quietly said, "Now go in there and tell them what you've done." He watched from the doorway as I returned the rocks at the nearby register and told the cashier I had taken them. She looked knowingly at Grandpa and said, "Thanks for returning them. You shouldn't steal things you know."

I knew.

What Grandpa did next will be forever etched in my mind and spirit. I fully expected a whoopin', the kind I got at home for lying. But

Grandpa had other plans. I was scared to go back to the door where he waited, but equally scared to stay in the store where the cashier had just learned of my crime. So I hung my head and walked toward Grandpa. When I got to the doorway where he stood, he held out his hand and said, "Let's go for a walk."

We walked quietly for a half a block or so away from the car. This seemed odd to me and then even odder when Grandpa led me into the local Dairy Queen and bought me a small strawberry sundae. He sat me down and started talking with me. He told me he liked polished rocks too and we made a plan together for how I could earn the money to buy some the next time we came to town. I don't remember any lecture about how bad I'd been or how wrong it was to steal and lie. For the first time I can remember, I was shown grace and love when I deserved the opposite. While I continued to struggle with lying and cheating as a youngster, I never did it again when I was in Grandpa's care. He empathized. He showed love. It changed me.

"You are capable"—What might help my child be successful and/or avoid misbehavior?

As referenced above, research has convincingly shown that helping children understand the benefits of telling the truth is a far more powerful motivator than scaring them about the dangers of lying. To encourage truth-telling, tell stories from your own life about times you told the truth even when you were tempted to lie. Let the kids know how good it feels to not have to keep the lie inside and to keep lying to cover up.

Parents tend to set their kids up to lie by asking them about something they know the child would want to hide from them. This can be very discouraging for the child, especially if the parent then punishes the child. It feels to the child like entrapment and causes the child to be less trusting of the parent. So when you know your child is having a hard time telling the truth, find ways and even create ways to "catch" your child telling the truth. Instead of asking "Did you brush your teeth?" say, "Let's quick check your toothbrush before you leave. Do you think I'll find it wet or dry?" The child will almost certainly tell the truth because there is no longer the option of getting away with anything. This is a much more encouraging approach and shows the child you are for him in the challenge of learning to tell more truth instead of against him in the battle to catch and punish lies.

Then, when the child says, "It's still dry." You can respond by affirming the true answer. Something like this: "You could have lied about that but you didn't. When you speak truth like this it helps me trust you more. Thanks! I really appreciate that."

Parents can also help children learn to value honesty as they "catch" them telling the truth without prompting. Kids tell the truth much more often than they lie. Listen to a child tell a story about her day. While she may slip in a stretch of truth or skip a detail here or there, you'll get a pretty accurate report about the day. Ask a child his favorite food or color or vacation and he'll tell the truth every time. Ask further about what was the best part of the trip, or day, or meal, and you'll get the truth. Any time you hear truth you have a chance to affirm, "You're telling the truth, aren't you? It feels good to tell the truth, doesn't it?"

You are responsible—What consequence best teaches my child responsibility for his actions?

Practice a right response: The first lies usually show up in two-year-old children. An interaction might go something like this: "Honey, did you mess your diaper?" Somehow children already have a sense that this is a problem, either because they feel ashamed about it (based on how they get treated when they need a diaper change) or because they'd rather not stop what they are doing to have their private parts exposed to the open air. So they lie. "No."

The way to encourage them to be truthful is to be sure there is a big, expressive reward for telling the truth. So stage a do-over and practice a truthful response. "Honey, I'm going to look in your diaper now. What is in there?" Now the child knows you're going to look and will likely say, "poopy." If not, you can prompt it like this, "Can you say poopy?" When the child says, "poopy," give some big, expressive energy and say, "That's right! You told me the truth!"

Lose the privilege: As kids get older their lies become more crafty. Certainly if the lie is about use of a privilege, i.e., screen time, car use, curfew, etc., then a consequence of the loss of that privilege is appropriate. But with craftier lying comes a deeper layer of issues to address.

Make restitution/reconcile: The most important part of lying is about relationship. Trust is broken and confessions and forgiveness are needed for restoration. So the most important consequences are about restoring the relationship and reconnecting in some way. Since children tend to lie less when they feel closely connected to someone, a possible consequence would be that the child needs to plan an outing to reconnect with the parent he deceived. One dad gave a consequence to his daughter that if he caught her in a lie, she was grounded until she reconnected with him by sharing something that she hadn't ever told anyone. This unusual consequence communicated that his priority was closeness and trust with her.

Aggression and Disrespect

Few things push parents' buttons like an aggressive, disrespectful child. When the button is pushed parents typically become energized to immediately control such behavior. They often shift into their most dominating posture and angrily proclaim, "Don't you dare talk to me that way!" or, "You can't treat your sister like that!" or, "Go to your room right now!" These anger-energized responses set an example that children are sure to follow. So the very behavior the parent is trying to curb is actually being reinforced.

Some parents wilt away from their kid's outbursts. This teaches kids that they are in charge. Allowing a child to dominate is no more constructive than dominating the child. A child who acts aggressively is making bad choices and ought to be held accountable for them. If a parent either backs away, or charges in to attempt to control the behavior, the child will not become truly accountable, and will not develop the heart of compassion and kindness toward others that parents desire.

However, when parents have both the confidence and self-control to thoughtfully and spiritually address what's going on, their children will feel more respected and will be more responsive to discipline. It is not quick, "Now say you're sorry!" kind of work; that simply teaches a child to avoid the hard work of true reconciliation in order to get out of trouble. It's tough work, that requires thoughtful preparation and vision in order to patiently dig through the complexities of each unique situation. The thoughtful parent's goal is not immediate control, but the goals of helping a child identify and honestly communicate his difficult feelings, understand the other person's point of view, and grow in skills for healthy and God-honoring conflict resolution; all with the love and grace of God permeating the whole process.

When learning how to help our children resolve conflicts with true respectfulness, it helps to understand a bit about brain function.

We know that children's brains can't access skills they don't have. This is a huge part of the problem with disrespect. Kids have not been taught the proper skills for conflict resolution, but parents somehow magically expect them to know how to respectfully resolve conflict. Much practice is needed, with supervision and affirmation, for kids to learn these deeply important skills. This practice helps establish the brain pathways used for conflict resolution.

Secondly, people in general, and particularly children, use "fight or flight" self-protection skills when they are angry, stressed, or feel threatened. These are basic functions needed when we are in danger. For efficient self-protection, the brain provides quick, easy access to bold aggressive or defensive responses, but blocks access to cognitive skills such as articulate language, awareness of feelings, or problem solving. Practically, this means that when a child is angry, he has *easy* access to aggressive responses like punch/shove or "You Dummyhead" and very limited access to "I'm angry that you took my truck. I feel disrespected, and I want it back." Attempting resolution when a child is really angry is pretty futile. A key strategy is to get calm first and communicate second.

Practical/Biblical rationale: Living relationships the way God intended is not about avoiding disrespect or even saying the "right" things. It's about walking in God's love and forgiveness for us, which frees us to honestly look into our own hearts. Then we can seek reconciliation and love others from a sincere heart of faith.

Consider these Scriptures:

> "Dear friends, since God so loved us, we also ought to love one another" (1 John 4:11).

"In your anger do not sin; when you are on your beds, search your hearts and be silent" (Psalm 4:4).

"Do not let any unwholesome talk come out of your mouths, but only what is helpful for building others up according to their needs, that it may benefit those who listen. Be kind and compassionate to one another, forgiving each other, just as in Christ God forgave you" (Eph. 4:29, 32).

"If your brother sins against you, go and show him his fault, just between the two of you" (Matt. 18:15).

"If you…remember that your brother or sister has something against you…go and be reconciled to them" (Matt. 5:23–24).

These two verses in Matthew's Gospel together indicate that regardless of who caused the conflict, both participants are responsible to initiate reconciliation. Think of the gossip, division, and bitterness that could be avoided in the Body of Christ if people were taught this clearly as children.

I prepare my heart—What's going on in me?

Consider these questions: Am I worried that I am raising a bully or fearful about what my child will be like as a teenager/spouse/parent? If my child lips off to me, do I instantly feel threatened? What's it like to be my child, right now? What does my child need to calm down and resolve this situation? What's the opportunity in this situation to build faith, character and skills? What can I do to prepare myself for these situations so I can stay peaceful?

You are loved—How can I connect or empathize?

Does my child know that I understand how hard it is to be really angry? Feeling truly understood takes the intensity out of anger because anger is about self-protection, usually a me-against-the-world emotion. A coaching client recently stated, "I've had so much less difficulty with Adam since our last session. I think it's because I had an epiphany about the power of really letting him know that I understand what he's feeling."

Carla looked beneath the surface of her adopted daughter, Tina's, anger and hurtful words, "I don't really love you!" Carla recognized this was progress from previous years when Tina would lash out physically or scream, "I hate you! You are a terrible mother!" She also knew that Tina was very anxious about an upcoming trip and she was masking that anxiety with the more powerful emotion of anger. Carla gently stated what was true, "Tina, I know you really do love me, just like I really love you." Then she compassionately and strongly added, "But you are really angry right now." Later Tina spontaneously apologized and restated her love for her mom, and they were able to talk about the anxiety under the anger.

"You are capable"—What might help my child be successful and/or avoid misbehavior?

Parents dealing with blatant disrespect/aggression often want their child to use calm, adult-like behaviors when they are angry. When the child doesn't have the skills or his brain is incapable of accessing those skills in his present state, the temptation is to tell him what to say or dictate the solutions that will put an immediate end to the situation. What does the child then learn? He likely learns that he is incapable and needs you to reconcile his conflicts and solve his problems. Hmm. It's probably not what you want him to learn. Just like learning to walk or to write their name, learning the conflict-resolution skills that can replace disrespect is a gradual process with lots of falls or messes along the way. But nearly every child can learn them if repeatedly given opportunities in a helpful, encouraging way.

Here are three important conflict resolutions skills children can practice and learn:

1. Self-calm, learn to take a break if needed
2. Understand the feelings and perspectives involved in the conflict
3. Problem-solve potential win-win solutions/compromises

Working on these skills helps a child to form an identity as a learner and a reconciler instead of as a troublemaker or aggressor. It helps parents and children alike become more accountable to constructive conflict resolution as they grow in confidence and experience. You can teach your children this simple sequence of conflict resolution principles and verses that apply:

1. Calm down

> "In your anger do not sin; when you are on your beds, search your hearts and be silent" (Psa. 4:4).

> "Anyone who is careful about what he says keeps himself out of trouble" (Pro. 21:23, NIRV).

2. Understand each other

> "…be quick to listen, slow to speak" (James 1:19).

> "…speak the truth in love" (Eph. 4:15, NIRV).

"Forgive one another as quickly and thoroughly as God in Christ forgave you" (Eph. 4:32).

3. Find a win-win

"then make my joy complete by being like-minded, having the same love, being one in spirit and of one mind. Do nothing out of selfish ambition or vain conceit. Rather, in humility value others above yourselves," (Phil. 2:2–3).

Once the children have learned these principles, you can come alongside them and coach them during conflict. Remind them of the principles and then engage in some of the ways described:

4. Help your child calm down by taking a break if needed.

- Guide the process without placing blame or judgment; model what you want your children to do. "Wow, you guys are pretty upset right now! Let's all take a little break to calm down and think about how to solve this problem." (Even if you aren't upset it gives you a chance to pray for wisdom.) Encourage your children to relax, take deep breaths, draw, run, remember a fun time together. You can remind your kids, "Jesus is right here and has plenty of peace and love for everybody."
- If children comply with taking a short calming break in a comfortable place, affirm how helpful and grown-up that is. This affirmation often changes the tone of the rest of the interaction. This break is not a timed punishment but a time to reflect and regroup. At other times, keep a watchful eye for any situation in which your child calms himself down. "Wow, you

started to get upset, and you calmed down. That was really cool! How'd you do that?" Even if they can't answer the question, it will get them thinking about it.

Tom had grown up in a strict, "I'm the dad so you do as I say, or else..." kind of home. Now as a parent he was frequently domineering and short-tempered, causing his son, Darren, to react with anger and defiance. He and his wife, Monica, really wanted to change the explosiveness in their home, so they tried a fun, short-term strategy to jump-start a new habit of calm conflict-resolution. Monica placed a few containers of small suckers around the house as a visual reminder to take a break and suck on the sucker to calm down before resolving conflict. This was particularly helpful for Monica and Darren, and made a notable improvement in their communication.

One day Tom was loud and upset but Darren was unusually calm. He sweetly offered, "Dad, you look a little upset. Do you want a sucker?" Despite Darren's positive approach, Tom felt that suckers were too juvenile for him. This tall, husky dad wasn't about to sit down with a little sucker! They decided to try something else, and strategically placed a couple of Post-it notes with a big "5" on them as reminders to take five deep breaths to calm down.

The post-it notes were somewhat helpful, but the real change for Tom came when they put up easy-to-read copies of James 1:19–20, "Everyone should be quick to listen, slow to speak and slow to become angry, because human anger does not produce the righteousness that God desires." He was passionate about God's righteousness filling their interactions (instead of selfishness and yelling), and this scripture gave him something to aspire to. At our next coaching session he described how he had stayed calm in their conflicts for the previous three weeks, with only one minor exception which he re-solved well. He was deeply pleased that he was no longer parent-ing the way he had been raised. Tom and Monica were very encour-aged at the fun, affection, and cooperation that now predominated their interactions with their son. These parents persevered to find the strategy that worked for their family. More importantly, their son saw God's word bring peace and joy to their home.

5. Help your child learn to identify and communicate feelings and understand other's feelings and perspectives.

- Young children need simple choices–"Are you sad or mad right now?" Older children can be invited to answer more complex questions like. "You seem upset. What's that about?" As you provide guidance, encourage kids by saying, "Remem-ber to be respectful when you tell us." In order to help your child to really try to understand her sibling's perspective, you can even have the kids write down what they feel and want, and then write down what they think the other person feels and wants, and compare notes. Challenge them to see how close they can get to writing the same thing, which will re-quire thoughtfulness and insight.
- If the conflict is with you, truly seek to understand your child first. This example will set the tone for getting through the conflict, and will usually open your child to hearing your per-spective. When you share your perspective, look for a chance to affirm a child's good listening *before* he starts to interrupt or contradict.
- Once children understand each other, parents can facilitate reconciliation by asking, "Is there anything you wish you'd

done differently?" which can then lead to, "Anything you'd like to apologize for?"

- Understanding other people's perspectives is sometimes very difficult for a child who is more intense, active or anxious than typical kids. If your child struggles with this, there are some great resources available at www.socialthinking.com. *You Are a Social Detective* is a great book for kids approximately ages five to ten years old that teaches them to figure out how their behavior affects other people and what those people think about them.

6. Find win-win situations by working together to create possible solutions and/or compromises.

- Remind younger children that part of growing up is thinking about everybody involved, not just themselves. "What's the one thing that's most important to each of you and how could your solution include those things?" Remind them of any previous successes at finding solutions.

Once this process becomes more familiar and normal (which can take a long time, so be patient!) children will begin to take more responsibility for their own resolution. When they conflict you can just ask with a smile, "Do you two need any help to resolve your conflict well?" This will help them anticipate success, want to be independent, and solve a problem on their own. Provide the least amount of help needed for them to be successful. A fun verse to prevent the unnecessary/unhelpful involvement of another person (yours or another sibling) is Proverbs 26:17: "Like one who seizes a dog by the ears is a passer-by who meddles in a quarrel not his own."

You are responsible—What consequence best teaches my child responsibility for his actions?

Small consequences are often enough. When a child uses a harsh tone or makes a disrespectful demand or statement, it may be suitable to just say in a relaxed manner, "That's a harsh way to express yourself. How might you say that respectfully?" When the child figures out a better way, you can tell her "That's much better. Now practice that a few times so it's easier to remember next time."

Bethany was quick to back little Noah up in conflicts with his intense older brother. Of course Daniel would feel ganged up on, and "Butt out, Bethany!" was his frequent harsh response. Over time he we helped him learn (through lots of repetition) to take a breath and say, "Bethany, this is not your issue."

When kids start to be disrespectful, a simple non-condemning, "Oops, how about a do-over?" can be all that is necessary for them to regroup and try a more respectful approach.

When the conflict has been more volatile, or led to deeper hurt in relationships, more is needed. Remember to stay respectful yourself as you navigate through this. Also remember that the ultimate goal of any consequences must be to help a child value and learn resolution skills. So when kids remain defiant, put some "loss of privilege" consequences with social implications in place that will compel them to go through restoration. Why? Because if you can't figure out how to resolve well with your own siblings, it will be hard for you to resolve well with others. For example:

For older kids:

- You can resume contact with your friends when you have done the hard work of reconciling.

241

- You can resume use of your computer or cell phone once you've resolved this well.
- You can go to the (game, mall, party, or whatever) when you get through this.

For younger kids:

- You can play with your sister again once you've worked this out.
- You can have the toys back (the ones that led to the conflict) once you've worked this out.
- You will wait in your room until you've settled down enough to work this out.

By now you're seeing that all of these consequences have yet another goal—to work things out! Far too often kids get punished for their disrespectful behavior in ways that don't lead to working things out. If things are not worked out, then conflict festers and emerges with more volatility over time. Scripture is strong about this. God has no desire for our worship or offerings until we have reconciled our conflicts. Matthew 5:23–24 says, "Therefore, if you are offering your gift at the altar and there remember that your brother or sister has something against you, leave your gift there in front of the altar. First go and be reconciled to them; then come and offer your gift."

A way to help teach children the value of a relationship is to communicate to them that "Your relationships are your first priority. If you have a conflict with someone, all other distracting activities are on hold until that conflict is resolved and you've reconciled well." Restricting these privileges in this way encourages children to reconcile but doesn't demand it immediately when they aren't ready. These consequences make good sense to children *if* parents proactively talk about reconciliation as a family value and model it themselves.

"Working it out"

Once the consequences that move kids toward "working it out" are in place, the child(ren) can wait until they are ready. They get to make this call. When they do, parents need skills for coming along side their children to facilitate conflict resolution. This is not for the faint of heart. Conflict is perhaps the hardest of dynamics to enter peacefully, purposefully, and constructively. Lynne and I have many times started well only to be drawn into unhelpful emotions and dynamics. But having a strategy and practicing it over and over again have strengthened us to dive in and stay the course.

The first important lesson we learned along the way is to avoid the typical approach, which is to give our biggest energy to the offender in sibling skirmishes. In the famous section of scripture regarding conflict resolution, Jesus' instructions are aimed at empowering victims. Matthew 18:15, 16 says, "If your brother sins against you, go and show him his fault, just between the two of you. If he listens to you, you have won your brother over. But if he will not listen, take one or two others along, so that 'every matter may be established by the testimony of two or three witnesses...'" The emphasis here is not on punishing the one who sinned, but on supporting the victim to confront the sinner, with as much assistance as needed. The goal of the process is the unforced repentance of the sinner. When my first response is to comfort and strengthen the victim, I build skills and values for resolving conflicts, while avoiding the reward of primary attention given to the aggressor.

The second important lesson is that imposed consequences are constructive only to the degree that they move kids toward a heartfelt apology and forgiveness. So right along with the consequences we put in place in the Jackson household, we put teaching in place about general principles of reconciliation. "If you used your hands to hurt, you can reconcile by using your hands to help," and, "It takes several healing statements to resolve a hurtful statement." (Lynne had learned in a seminar that it takes four positive statements to counteract the impact of one negative statement.) We taught our kids directly from the Bible as part of their discipleship for resolution. One of our favorite passages, spoken often, was Proverbs 12:18, "Reckless words pierce like a sword, but the tongue of the wise brings healing." When children are reckless, give them a chance to be wise as part of their consequence.

Here are a couple other restitution consequences we put in place:

- The consequence for physical aggression was that all distracting privileges are on hold until you have resolved this problem by doing something kind for the one you hurt or threatened.
- For name-calling or strong verbal disrespect (something unkind and untrue), the reconciliation was four statements that were both kind and true, including setting the untruth straight. (You're not a Stupidbutt!) At least two of the statements had to be fresh, creative statements. Sometimes the "Four Kind and Trues" included some pretty silly stuff (Your eyes match; You're not an alien), and occasionally if the offending sibling got stuck for new ideas the "victim" helped out by suggesting something. This process often set the tone for some good fun and connection afterward.

One day at dinner when Lynne was irritated and sarcastic with

Daniel, he launched a couple of explosive zingers back at her. After she apologized for her part of the conflict, his reconciliation consequence was to write down eight "Kind and Trues" for her: "You are not a nincompoop; You are not a sarcastic piece of feces; I love you; You rock the house; You are very tolerant; You da woman!; Thank you for the meal; You make good food." Finding that piece of paper years later was quite entertaining.

Our children came to increasingly value this process as we helped them notice the joy that came with true reconciliation contrasted with how the conflict felt before it was resolved. We used these times to discuss the forgiving and reconciling nature of God. This is yet another example of how we discipled our children through our discipline.

What was the fruit of all this effort? We are deeply blessed by watching the healthy, compassionate way our kids relate to others. As a young adult Daniel stated, "I love apologizing, because I can take the wrong I've done, cast it off and be free of it and have it be forgiven by both God and man. It's beautiful!"

NOTES

APPENDIX B

1. The Institute for American Values, Hardwired to Connect, The New Scientific Case for Authoritative Communities, (New York: 2003). pp. 31, 38, 39.

APPENDIX C

1. http://www.npr.org/blogs/health/2011/12/05/143062378/whats-behind-a-temper-tantrum-scientists-deconstruct-the-screams
2. Dr. Harvey Karp, The Happiest Toddler on the Block, DVD, 2010
3. Po Bronson, Learning to Lie, http://nymag.com/news/features/43893/index4.html, Feb 10, 2008

REFERENCES

Bronson, Po. "Learning to Lie," http://nymag.com/news/features/43893./index4.html, published Feb 10, 2008, viewed 12/16/08.

Hardel, Richard A and Merton P. Strommen, *Passing On the Faith* , Winona, MN: Christian Brothers Publications. 2000.

Hardwired to Connect, The New Scientific Case for Authoritative Communities. The Institute for American Values, New York: 2003.

Heath, Chip and Dan Heath; *Switch, How to Change Things When Change Is Hard*, New York: Random House, Inc. 2010.

McDonald, Angie. *Attachment to God and Parents: Testing the Correspondence vs. Compensation Hypotheses*, Journal of Psychology and Christianity, Vol. 24, No. 1. 2005.